Digital Painting in Photoshop

Digital Painting in Photoshop

Susan Ruddick Bloom

ELSEVIER

AMSTERDAM • BOSTON • HEIDELBERG • LONDON
NEW YORK • OXFORD • PARIS • SAN DIEGO
SAN FRANCISCO • SINGAPORE • SYDNEY • TOKYO
Focal Press is an imprint of Elsevier

Focal
Press

Focal Press is an imprint of Elsevier
30 Corporate Drive, Suite 400, Burlington, MA 01803, USA
Linacre House, Jordan Hill, Oxford OX2 8DP, UK

Library of Congress Cataloging-in-Publication Data
Application submitted

British Library Cataloguing-in-Publication Data
A catalogue record for this book is available from the British Library.

ISBN: 978-0-240-81114-7

For information on all Focal Press publications
visit our website at www.elsevierdirect.com

09 10 11 12 5 4 3 2 1

Printed in Canada

To Anne Marie, our first grandchild. You have brought joy and wonder into our lives.

Contents

Contents

CHAPTER 1

Introduction to the Concept of Digital Painting

Humankind has felt the urge to paint since the dawn of time. Over the centuries our painting materials have varied. We have used oil as a binder to hold crushed minerals together. We have used water as a vehicle to spread pigments. Even wax has been used for centuries in a technique called encaustics. Most of these methods rely on the ground-up fragments of minerals and rocks. Modern paints have introduced new colors through the use of chemical technology.

Our palettes have changed over time because of the types of materials that were currently available. The colors available to Warhol were not available to Monet. The colors used by Van Gogh were not available to Michelangelo. In short, our materials dictate the limitations and opportunities that we, as artists, work under.

This book will offer techniques for the new field of digital painting. We will be pushing pixels instead of pigment. Our canvas is our monitor. Our palette

FIG. 1-1 Digital pastel of a garden bridge.

will be described in terms such as RGB, CMYK, and the catch-all term of color space. Our work, when completed, will be printed, returning it to the world of pigments. The types of pigments used in digital printing are changing rapidly. There are dye-based inks and pigment-based inks, not to mention dye sublimation printing. It is reasonable to assume that the technology will continue to change. In response, our painting techniques will also change.

This book is directed at a diverse population. I imagine that photographers will use this book to create unique hand-painted images from their photographs. Studios may find that a painterly approach may differentiate their work from their competitors. These approaches can be used on everything from a landscape to a portrait to a still life. The possibilities are virtually endless. Artists may use this book for a new and fresh approach to painting. They may decide to dig into a digital painting with just a sketch or a concept. They may choose to work from a photograph as a reference. Illustrators may use these techniques to render different effects. College professors may use this book as a text in a course dedicated to digital fine art.

Throughout the book I will be using my own photographs, and unless I state otherwise I will be using a resolution of 300 dpi. I am comfortable with the quality of that resolution for printing fine art and it is the standard for my work.

I always recommend that you work on your own images. You will not fall afoul of copyright issues if you confine your artistic endeavors to your own imagery. We each see with a different eye. The completed piece of art should be yours through and through. I'm always astounded, as I take photographers on photo trips abroad, at how unique each person's vision truly is. We visit the same locales, stand in virtually the same spots, but each photographer's imagery is quite different from the others'. Trust your instinct and your creative eye. Use your own imagery, as it will bring you greater joy and fulfillment.

I do not attempt to cover the field of color management or printing know-how in this book. Each of those topics deserves a book of its own. I may, from time to time, suggest possible ways I might consider printing a particular piece, often matching the type of paper to the technique involved. For example, I might suggest printing a digital oil painting on a canvas substrate. For the pastel approach I might suggest a heavy paper with a texture. But how to print your piece is a judgment call, and the decision is yours and yours alone. Some of you might possess high-end ink-jet printers and do your own printing. Some of you may choose to send your files out to a service provider that has a high-quality printer.

Very large pieces are in vogue now. Large work requires a certain expertise, and very large pieces require more than one person to handle them. If you choose to work very large you will most likely send your work out for printing and framing. Choose a framer that is experienced in digital prints. Prints need to "de-gas" for several days, expelling chemicals from the printing process, before they are encased in a frame.

How do you select the photographs that will be rendered into a painting? This is a mysterious process indeed. It sounds wacky to say that the right images "speak" to me, but that is what happens. Before you call the men in little white coats, I should say I don't really hear voices. Rather, I notice something about the image that suggests a certain rendering technique. As the artist, you need to be attentive to the nature of the image. What kind of mood or effect does it suggest to you? Some images suggest a lighter, more transparent medium, while others would look better with an opaque paint that leaves brush marks.

One of the best things that you can do to make yourself more knowledgeable about these art techniques is to frequently go to museums. Study the work. Get close to the canvas or paper and study the brushwork, color palette employed, composition, and the nature of the medium (oil, pastels, charcoals, watercolors, etc.). The more you understand about the medium, the more successful your digital versions will be.

Another suggestion that I like to give my students is to give yourself the gift of time. Block aside a certain amount of time every week that you devote to developing your digital skills. Mastery requires practice, whether your subject is the piano, tennis, the stock market, or surgery. You must give yourself the time to really explore these techniques.

Allow yourself the luxury of making mistakes and then forgive yourself and move on. Making mistakes is a great way to learn. There is no shortcut to perfection. Although mistakes in surgery can be deadly, mistakes in digital art can be valuable. There is not a digital police force to reign you in. Go for it. Experiment. Play like a child with a new box of crayons. You don't have to play by my rules or those of anyone else. You can draw on top of a digital painting. You can draw on your paper before you print on it. You can collage over your digital painting. It is your art, and you are the person that must decide where your art will take you.

I wish you the best on this artistic digital ride. May your imagery give you personal joy, and may the process of creating digital art be challenging and satisfying to your spirit. My techniques should be just a starting point for you. Try not to be too literal about following every stroke that I illustrate. Trust your instincts. Take off that digital seat belt, let those artistic breezes blow through your hair, and go out and make art!

The Basic Tools for Painting in Photoshop

The techniques employed in this book have several things in common. There are basic tools and concepts that are used throughout the book. These tools and why they are important are laid out for you here in Chapter 2, as a reference.

Photoshop has many wonderful tools that can be used for painting, but they are often ignored, misunderstood, or hidden. The hidden ones are usually hiding in plain sight. They are the tools that you may have never tried. You know the ones; like the glowing edges filter. What in the world would you use that wacky filter for? It sports neon colors and a black background. What were the software engineers thinking? I'll show you how that crazy filter can be your ticket to great sketches.

Photoshop is awash in wonderful brushes, but most users never go past the basic brushes to the libraries full of great brush tools. We will also explore making your own brushes from scratch. The same is true of textures.

FIG. 2-1 Digital painting of a water lily.

Photoshop has dozens of textures that can be applied to your work, giving a textural feel like canvas or the look of a handmade paper. The textures are a bit more hidden but very accessible when you realize their intrinsic value. Again, we will look at how you can create your own textures.

Last, there are great tool techniques that you can learn using the Art History Brush, the History Brush, and the Pattern Stamp Brush. These tools can greatly aid you on your painterly quest.

Brushes

Lots of tools are called brushes. The brush is a brush, of course, but so is the Clone tool. The eraser is a brush. We use brushes on our masks. Photoshop is full of brushes. Most Photoshop users know that there are hard brushes and soft brushes. The hard brushes have a hard, concrete edge, with no feathering. You can control the softness of the edge in the brush dynamics, under Hardness.

This is similar to the feather used in the Rectangular and Elliptical Marquee tools. A feather of 0 yields a solid edge. A feather of 40 yields a soft edge. A feather of 80 yields a very soft edge. This technique is good for vignetting a photo. The amount of feather needed will be determined by the size and resolution of the targeted file. Larger files contain more pixels and will need a higher feather amount to achieve a very soft edge.

Brushes are critical for how a mark is laid down. The softness of the edge is important, but beyond that, the primary consideration is the texture of the mark. Photoshop has libraries full of brushes. They can be viewed by clicking on the triangle at the upper right corner.

The Default Brush menu offers a huge array of brushes, even one for your cat, entitled Fuzzball. Some are bizarre and some are quite useful.

As a convenience for you, I've created a reference section containing all the various Brush Libraries and the brush names and the type of stroke that they make. They are listed here in the order that they appear in the Photoshop menu. I hope it saves time for you, as you search for just that right brush.

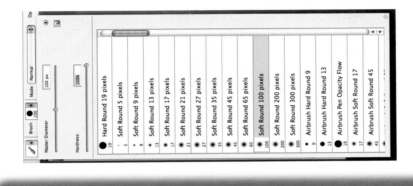

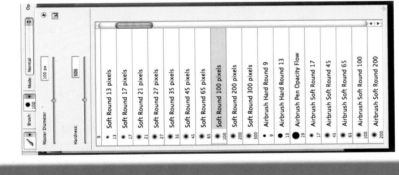

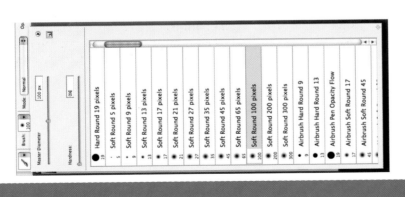

FIG. 2-2 Left: 100% hardness; middle: 50% hardness; right: 0% hardness.

FIG. 2-3 Left: 0 feather; middle: 40 pixel feather; right: 80 pixel feather, using the Elliptical Marquee tool.

That covers the brushes that come embedded in various Brush Libraries in Photoshop. However, there are more brushes to explore. You can gather more brushes from various Internet sites, many of them free, or you can craft your own brush from scratch. It is so easy, and no one will have a brush just like yours.

When thinking about what characteristics you want your brush to possess, consider the type of medium that you are working with. Watercolor artists use soft sable brushes to handle that thin layer of pigment suspended in water. Oil paints require a much sturdier brush. The bristles on an oil painting brush are generally coarse and thick. They are often made from pig or ox hair. An oil painting brush needs strength and durability to move thick oil paint around. This type of brush frequently leaves marks in the paint, showing the tracks of those coarse bristles. Pastels and charcoal are dry painting mediums. They leave their pigment deposits on paper that has texture, known as "tooth." The mark that these dry mediums leave behind is rough, especially on the edges, but occasionally with gaps in the mark itself. They have vacant or small empty areas where the paper shows through the mark. The choice of a brush is a major factor when beginning a digital painting.

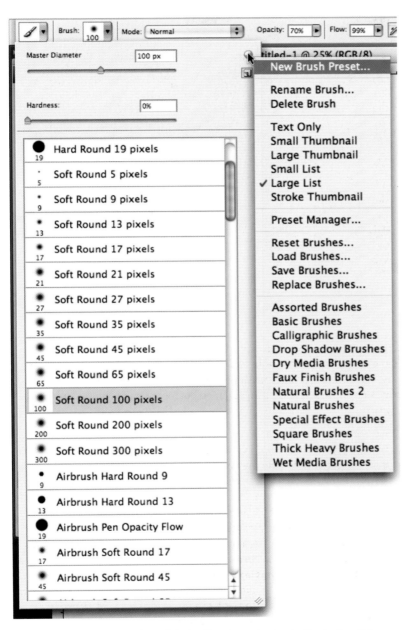

FIG. 2-4 Menu that reveals Brush Libraries (below) and how they can be viewed as thumbnails and lists.

Default Brushes

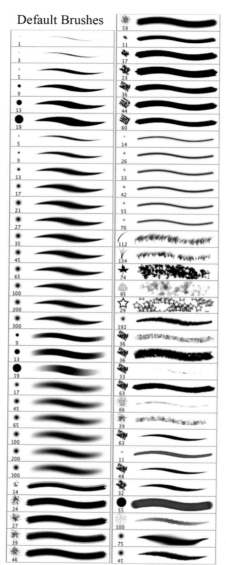

Hard Round 1 Pixel	Spatter 59 Pixels
Hard Round 3 Pixels	Chalk 11 Pixels
Hard Round 5 Pixels	Chalk 17 Pixels
Hard Round 9 Pixels	Chalk 23 Pixels
Hard Round 13 Pixels	Chalk 36 Pixels
Hard Round 19 Pixels	Chalk 44 Pixels
Soft Round 5 Pixels	Chalk 60 Pixels
Soft Round 9 Pixels	Star 14 Pixels
Soft Round 13 Pixels	Star 26 Pixels
Soft Round 17 Pixels	Star 33 Pixels
Soft Round 21 Pixels	Star 42 Pixels
Soft Round 27 Pixels	Star 55 Pixels
Soft Round 35 Pixels	Star 70 Pixels
Soft Round 45 Pixels	Dune Grass
Soft Round 65 Pixels	Grass
Soft Round 100 Pixels	Scattered Maple Leaves
Soft Round 200 Pixels	Scattered Leaves
Soft Round 300 Pixels	Flowing Stars
Airbrush Hard Round 9 pixels	Fuzzball
Airbrush Hard Round 13 pixels	Chalk
Airbrush Pen Opacity Flow	Charcoal Large Smear
Airbrush Soft Round 17	Hard Pastel on Canvas
Airbrush Soft Round 45	Oil Pastel Large
Airbrush Soft Round 65	Dry Brush Tip Light Flow
Airbrush Soft Round 100	Dry Brush
Airbrush Soft Round 200	Watercolor Loaded Wet Flat Tip
Airbrush Soft Round 300	Watercolor Small Round Tip
Spatter 14 Pixels	Oil Heavy Flow Dry Edges
Spatter 24 Pixels	Oil Medium Wet Flow
Spatter 27 Pixels	Wet Sponge
Spatter 39 Pixels	Rough Round Bristle
Spatter 46 Pixels	Airbrush75 Tilt Size and Angle
	Airbrush Dual Brush Soft Round 45

FIG. 2-5 Default Brush menu.

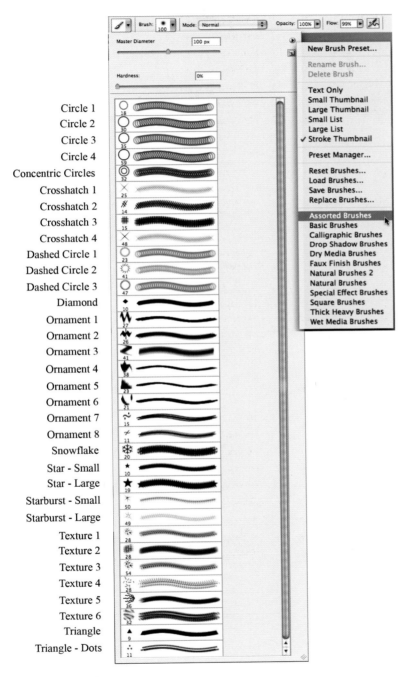

FIG. 2-6 Assorted brushes.

Hard Mechanical 1 pixel
Hard Mechanical 2 pixels
Hard Mechanical 3 pixels
Hard Mechanical 4 pixels
Hard Mechanical 5 pixels
Hard Mechanical 6 pixels
Hard Mechanical 7 pixels
Hard Mechanical 9 pixels
Hard Mechanical 12 pixels
Hard Mechanical 13 pixels
Hard Mechanical 16 pixels
Hard Mechanical 18 pixels
Hard Mechanical 19 pixels
Hard Mechanical 24 pixels
Hard Mechanical 28 pixels
Hard Mechanical 32 pixels
Hard Mechanical 36 pixels
Hard Mechanical 38 pixels
Hard Mechanical 48 pixels
Hard Mechanical 60 pixels
Soft Mechanical 1 pixel
Soft Mechanical 2 pixels
Soft Mechanical 3 pixels
Soft Mechanical 4 pixels
Soft Mechanical 5 pixels
Soft Mechanical 7 pixels
Soft Mechanical 9 pixels
Soft Mechanical 12 pixels
Soft Mechanical 13 pixels
Soft Mechanical 14 pixels
Soft Mechanical 16 pixels
Soft Mechanical 17 pixels
Soft Mechanical 18 pixels
Soft Mechanical 21 pixels
Soft Mechanical 24 pixels
Soft Mechanical 28 pixels
Soft Mechanical 35 pixels
Soft Mechanical 45 pixels
Soft Mechanical 48 pixels
Soft Mechanical 60 pixels
Soft Mechanical 65 pixels
Soft Mechanical 100 pixels
Soft Mechanical 300 pixels
Soft Mechanical 500 pixels

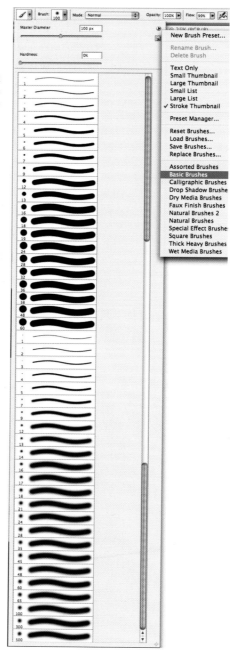

FIG. 2-7 Basic brushes.

Flat 6 pixels

Flat 10 pixels

Flat 15 pixels

Flat 20 pixels

Flat 28 pixels

Flat 35 pixels

Flat 45 pixels

Flat 60 pixels

Oval 7 pixels

Oval 10 pixels

Oval 15 pixels

Oval 20 pixels

Oval 28 pixels

Oval 35 pixels

Oval 45 pixels

Oval 60 pixels

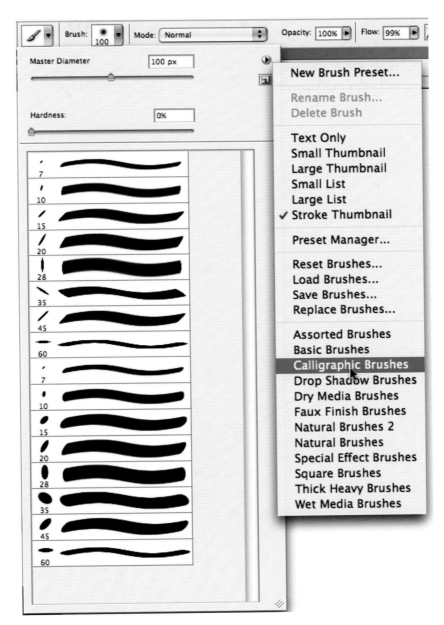

FIG. 2-8 Calligraphy brushes.

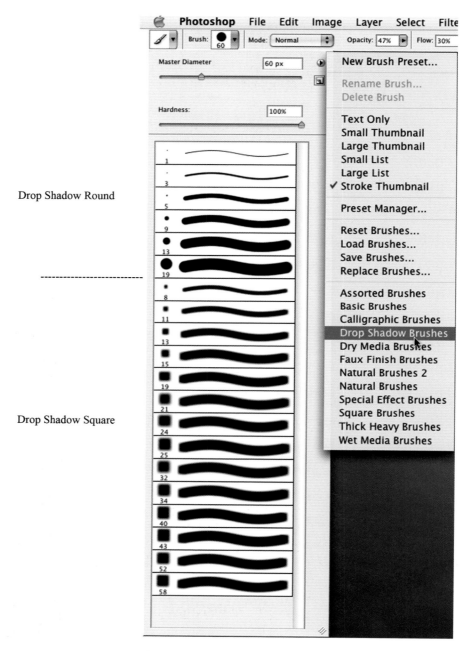

FIG. 2-9 Drop shadow brushes.

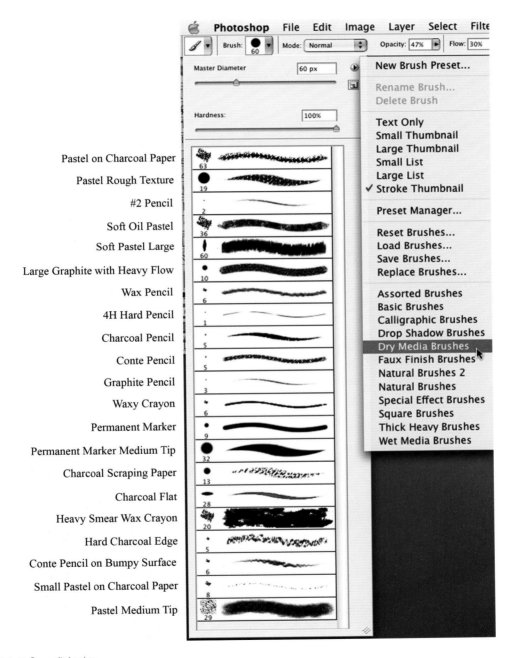

FIG. 2-10 Dry media brushes.

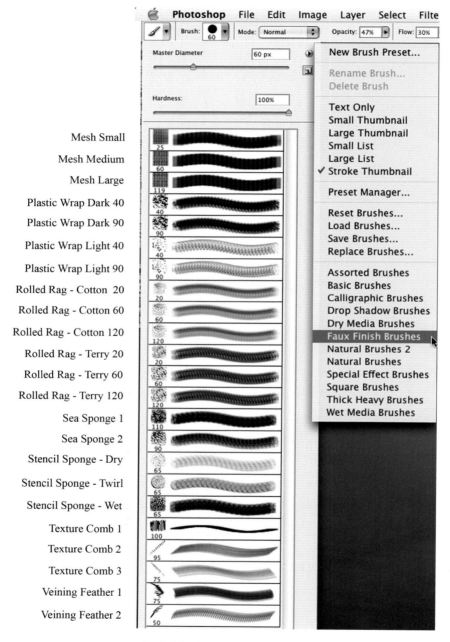

FIG. 2-11 Faux finish brushes.

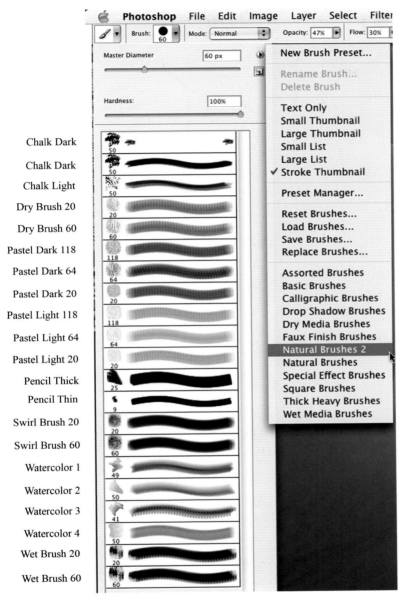

FIG. 2-12 Natural 2 brushes.

FIG. 2-13 Natural brushes.

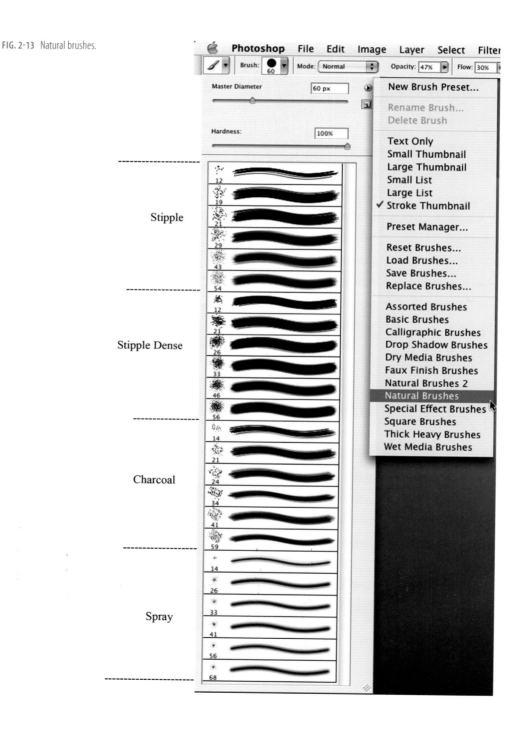

Stipple

Stipple Dense

Charcoal

Spray

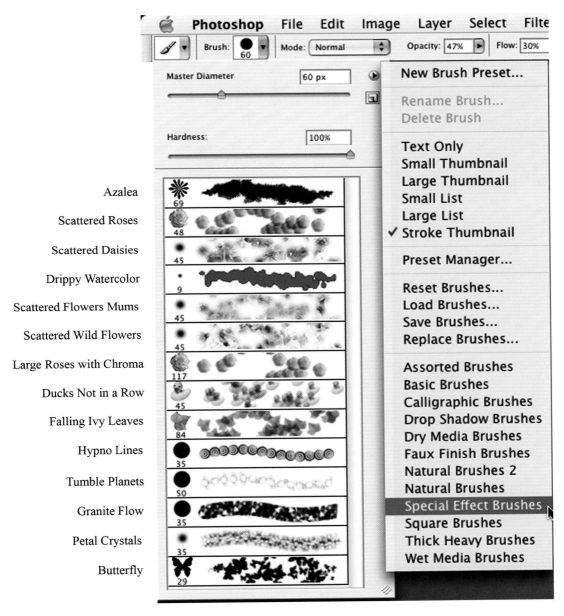

FIG. 2-14 Special effect brushes.

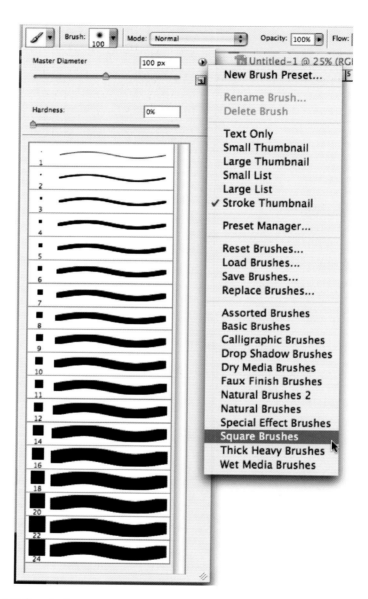

FIG. 2-15 Square brushes.

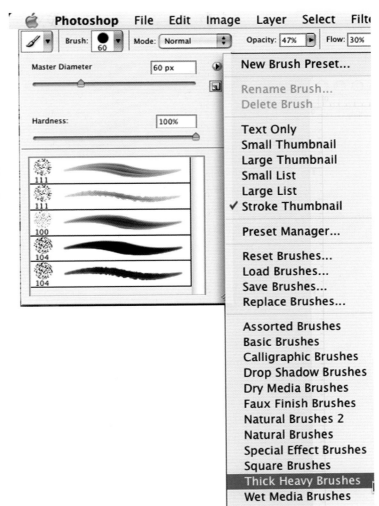

Flat Bristle

Rough Flat Bristle

Round Bristle

Smoother Round Bristle

Rough Round Bristle

FIG. 2-16 Thick heavy brushes.

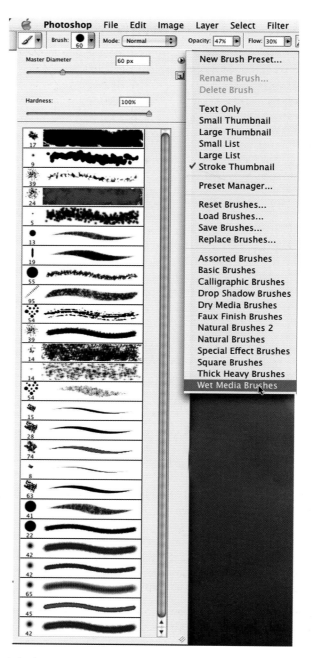

Rough Round Bristle
Drippy Water
Dry Brush on Towel
Heavy Scatter Flow
Heavy Stipple
Brush on Light Weave
Light Oil Flat Tip
Paint on Rough Texture
Paintbrush Tool Texture Comb
Rough Dry Brush
Rough Ink
Scattered Dry Brush
Scattered Dry Brush Small Tip
Large Texture Strokes
Oil Heavy Flow Small Tip
Brush with Thick Flow Medium Tip
Oil Medium Brush Wet Edges
Oil Small Tip
Oil Medium to Large Tip
Brush Light Texture Medium Tip
Watercolor Heavy Loaded
Watercolor Heavy Pigments
Watercolor Heavy Medium Tip
Watercolor Fat Tip
Watercolor Textured Surface
Watercolor Light Opacity

FIG. 2-17 Wet media brushes.

Making Your Own Brush

Making a brush in Photoshop is easy. For our example, I'll design a brush that has been abused. It will have loose, straggly hairs and leave a scratchy mark. I like this kind of brush for work with a dry medium, like charcoal or pastel. There is no reason to reinvent the whole wheel, or, in our case, brush. We will get a jump start by using an existing brush.

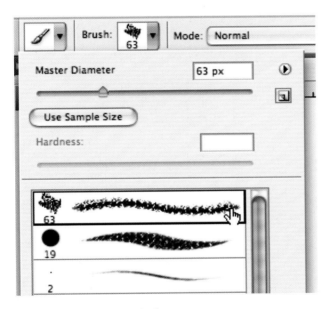

FIG. 2-18 Brush selected from the dry medium brushes.

I chose the top brush from the dry medium brushes. It is dark and scratchy and has vacant spots throughout the stroke, simulating bumpy paper.

This cluster of marks gives us the base for our own unique brush.

The next step is to get that loose, hairy look. To achieve that effect, use a 2 pixel brush to make both white-and-black marks over and through our beginning mark cluster. The possibilities are endless.

Next, using the Crop tool, remove excess white paper surrounding the mark. The brush will still be huge since I was using 300 dpi resolution. But that is okay, since Photoshop will do an excellent job of scaling the brush down to a smaller size when needed.

FIG. 2-19 Cluster a few marks together, leaving scratchy edges.

FIG. 2-20 Add black-and-white random lines.

FIG. 2-21 Cropping the brush shape.

FIG. 2-22 Define Brush Preset.

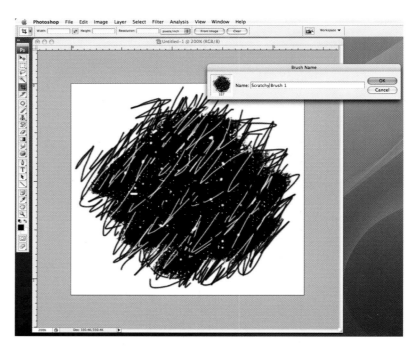

FIG. 2-23 Name your brush.

The next step is so simple. Just go to Edit – Define Brush Preset. This step is your ticket to making an endless number of unique brushes.

A dialogue box will appear with your new brush so that you can give it a name. Try to make the name descriptive of the type of mark the brush will make.

Your new brush will stay in the brush selections until you decide to remove it. You can see that my scratchy brush is huge, weighing in at 337 pixels. That is not a problem, as it is easy to request a smaller version of that brush by changing the Master Diameter slider on your brush controls.

You Can Make a Brush from Anything

You really can make a brush from just about anything. In this example, we'll use a Clone Stamp tool on a photograph of a stucco wall. I'm always photographing texture, wherever I find it. This photograph was taken in Italy. I'm sure the locals were dumbfounded to see a tourist taking a picture of the

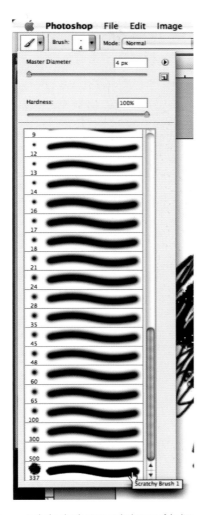

FIG. 2-24 Your brush will appear in the brush selections, at the bottom of the list.

wall, when fabulous statuary occupied the same plaza (I did photograph the fountain and statuary also).

Texture Libraries

I keep extensive files of texture to use with digital collages and patterns of texture at a later date. I highly recommend this practice. Take photographs of grass, stones, walls, hay, hair, wood, literally any texture. Drop those random

FIG. 2-25 Italian stucco wall.

images into a desktop folder. When the folder is getting large, burn a couple DVDs to add to your library of visual images.

We are visual artists, and as such, we need a visual vocabulary. It is important to build a visual library of images. This source material will prove beneficial in your artistic journey. It is so easy to carry a small digital camera with you everywhere. As you notice things of interest, photograph them. Download those images onto your computer and place them in special folders. Folders that sit on my desktop for later use include Textures, Flowers, Sky, and Water. When the folder is large enough, I burn a set of DVDs for archiving in two separate locations. It is always advisable to burn an extra copy as insurance for disk failure. I then empty the folder to make room for future images, to continue my visual library.

My aim here was to use the texture from the wall in a brush. I selected an area of texture in the photograph, using the Clone Stamp tool. The selected area was then "deposited" onto a blank white file. I think of these files as white sheets of paper.

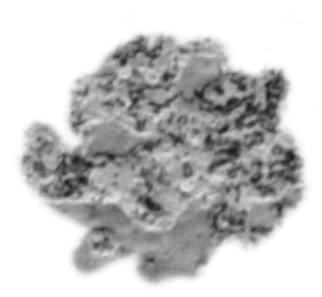

FIG. 2-26 "Deposit" of cloned stucco wall.

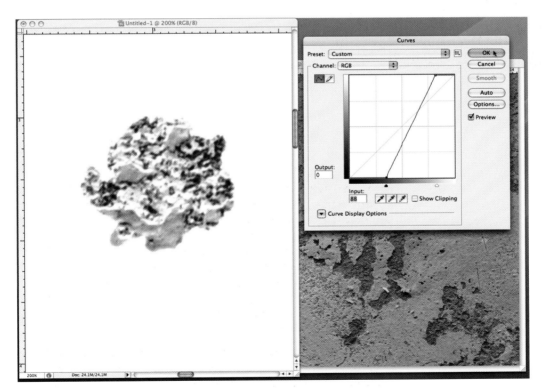

FIG. 2-27 Curves was used to create contrast.

The next step was to Edit – Adjustments – Desaturate, removing the color from the cloned sample. Once that step was completed, Curves was used to create more contrast. Both the black and the white points were moved toward the center (middle grey) to yield more contrast. Violà! You now have another distinctive mark to use in creating a brush preset. This technique could be used with practically any photograph and the Clone Stamp tool.

Brush Palette

But wait! Just when you thought we had surely exhausted all our brush possibilities, there are more. Photoshop has a Brush Palette that can be accessed from the Window menu. It looks a little daunting, at first, because it offers so many options. Let's explore some of those options together.

FIG. 2-28 Brush tip shape.

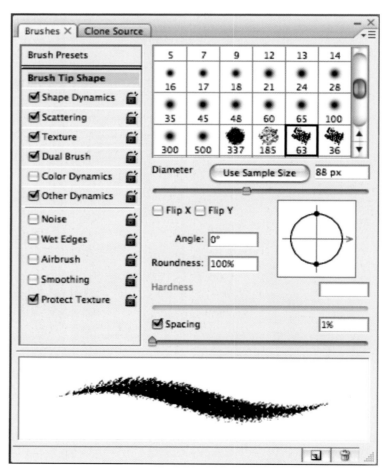

What is the shape of that brush? Is it full and round, or is it flat or tapered? This is where you decide on the look of your brush. In other words, you get to give your brush a hair style.

You can select an existing brush from the loaded Brush Libraries.

The Diameter slider will determine how narrow or wide your brush will be, measuring the diameter by pixels.

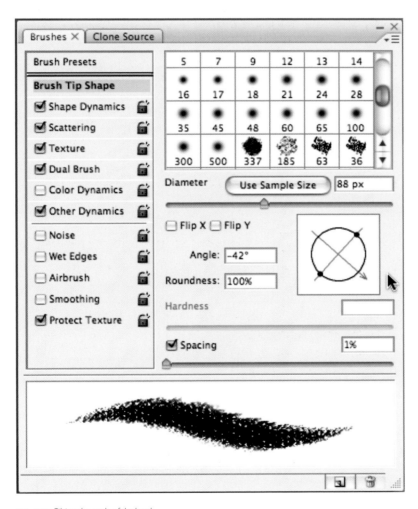

FIG. 2-29 Tilting the angle of the brush.

You can tilt the angle of your brush by degrees. Angled brushes give a chiseled look. You can flip the axis of horizontal or vertical orientation by checking the boxes labeled Flip X and Flip Y.

The Hardness slider controls the hardness of the center of the brush. Some existing brushes will not allow you to change this setting.

FIG. 2-30 Spacing slider causes the brush to "skip."

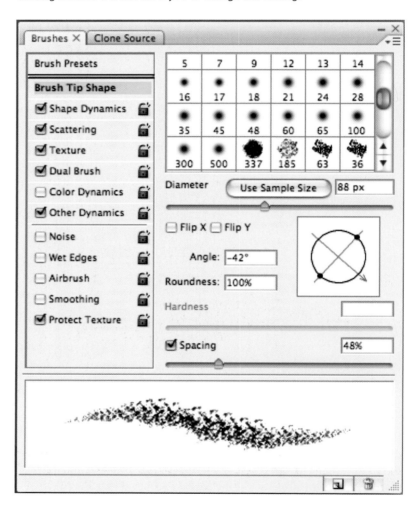

By moving the Spacing slider you can cause the brush to "skip."

Brush Shape Dynamics determines the variance of your brush marks in a stroke. The diameter will control the size. Again, you can control the X- and Y-axis. The angle jitter controls the variety of angles made by the marks in the

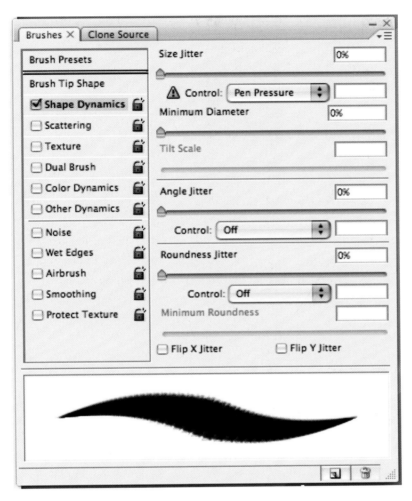

FIG. 2-31 Brush Shape Dynamics menu.

stroke. The roundness jitter is based on the ratio between the brush's long and short axes. Experiment with these sliders until you see the effect you want in your stroke.

The Scattering sliders control how brush marks are distributed in a stroke. Again, experiment with the Control sliders.

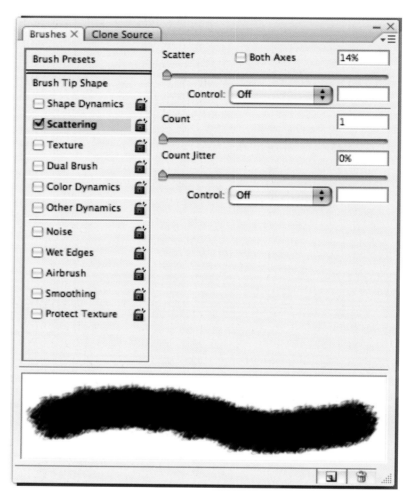

FIG. 2-32 Scattering controls.

The variables on the Texture Control sliders are practically without number.
Photoshop has tons of different patterns or textures in the Pattern Libraries. You
can simulate canvas, linen, wood, and more. Couple that with all the blending
modes available and add some jitter, and you will need a Ph.D. in mathematics

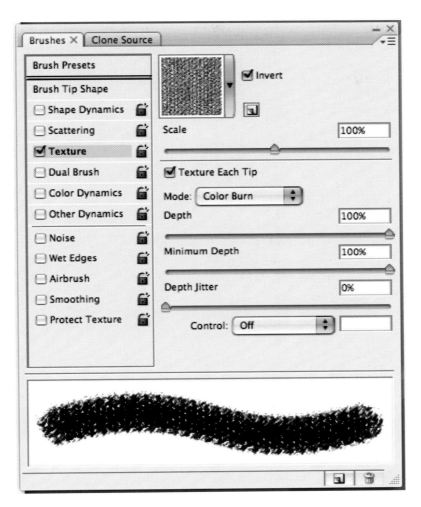

FIG. 2-33 Texture controls.

to calculate the variety of options you have. If you are like me, you can just move the sliders around on the texture you selected until you get the desired brush stroke. It is easy to get overwhelmed at all the choices.

Using dual brush control is like painting with two different brushes at once. The texture of brush two is incorporated in the primary brush selected, where

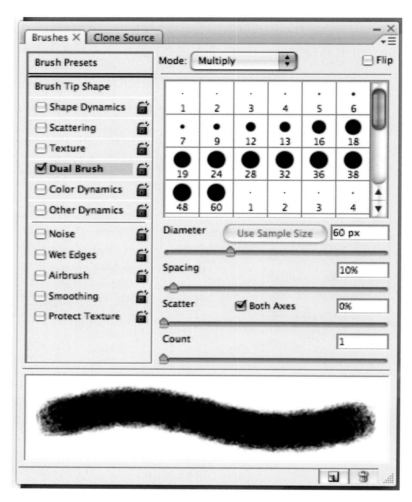

FIG. 2-34 Dual brush control.

the tips intersect. If you change the texture pattern, you get a different effect altogether.

Color Dynamics determines how the color will change during the course of the stroke. You can specify how the color of the stroke will vary from your foreground and background colors.

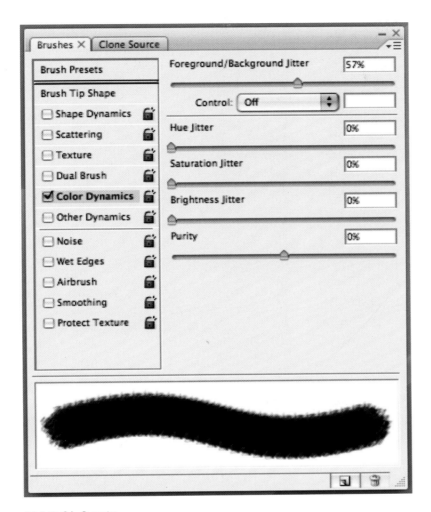

FIG. 2-35 Color Dynamics.

If those options are not enough for you, there are some more grouped under the title Other Dynamics. These sliders control how paint changes as the stroke is made.

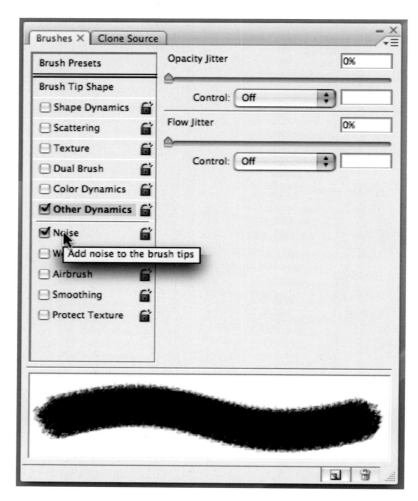

FIG. 2-36 Other Dynamics – Noise.

A randomness is added to the stroke, especially on the edges. With a Soft Edge Brush it may yield some mid-tones.

The Wet Edges Dynamics is a great brush effect. Remember this one! It will be essential in some of our digital watercolor effects.

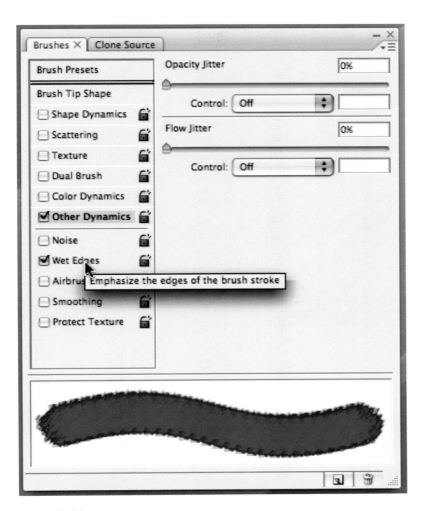

FIG. 2-37 Wet Edges.

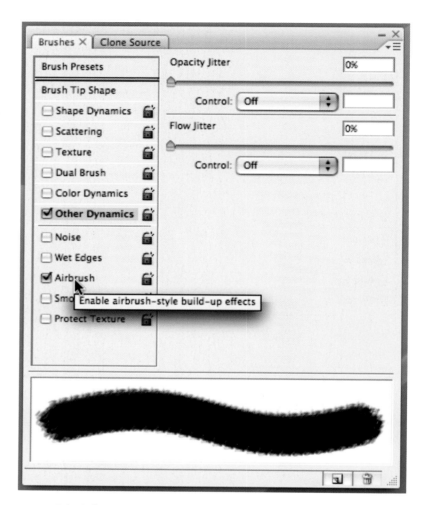

FIG. 2-38 Airbrush effect.

The Airbrush effect can build up like a traditional airbrush. Think graffiti, T-shirts made at the beach, or flames painted on a sports car. It has a soft edge and is often built with layers of application.

Smoothing is noticed most on the curves. A brush with smoothing may introduce a bit of lag time when painting quickly.

This creates a consistent textural effect, like canvas, when painting with textured brushes.

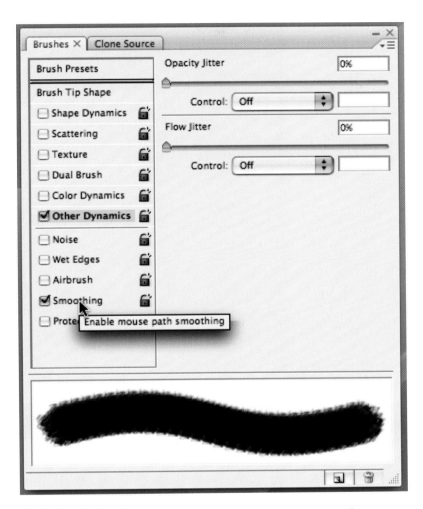

FIG. 2-39 Smoothing dynamics.

I hope you have fun exploring the myriad of brushes that are part of Photoshop. Try making your own brushes, and use the Brush menu to modify brushes. The brush you choose to work with has a huge impact on the quality and look of your digital painting.

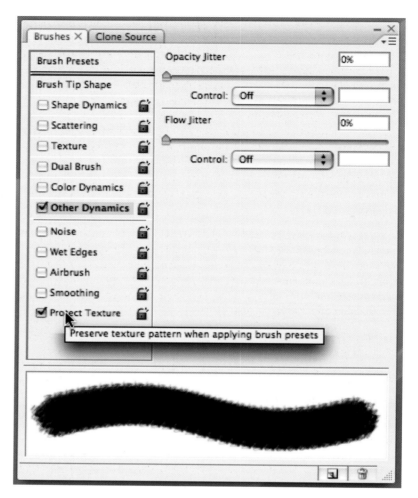

FIG. 2-40 Protect texture.

Patterns

Paintings have texture. If you look at an oil painting up close you can discover many things. Not only can you see the tracks from the brush, but you can often see the underlying canvas texture. This is especially true of paintings done on paper. Watercolors are most frequently done on a cold-press paper that has a bit of a textured bump. Some watercolor papers have a very pronounced, bumpy texture. Charcoal and pastel papers also have a texture, referred to as "tooth." This textured surface quite literally saws off the dust particles from the piece of chalk or charcoal.

As the field of digital fine art has exploded, we have been fortunate to see an increasing number of great papers available for our digital paintings. Many high-quality paper mills that produce fine artists' papers are now producing those same great papers with an inkjet coating. It is now possible to purchase textured inkjet paper made with good archival materials. You can purchase paper with cotton and rag content instead of wood by-products. A variety of thicknesses or paper weights are now available in several sizes and on rolls. Many manufacturers also make inkjet-coated canvas, that is, real canvas with a special coating, not just a paper imprinted with a faux canvas texture. Beautiful Japanese papers with inkjet coatings can also be found. Some are incredibly thin and somewhat transparent. Some have fibers or flowers or leaves embedded in the paper. The choices are ever-expanding and so exciting.

Another possibility for digital paintings is to apply an inkjet coating to the art paper of your choice. I've experimented with inkaid (http://www.inkaid.com) and liked the results. These inkjet products can be applied to paper, canvas, fabric, and even aluminum. A new entrant into the self-applied inkjet coating market is Golden (http://www.goldenpaints.com/mixmoremedia/index.php). Their products are also very good.

As I stated in Chapter 1, this book will not cover the increasingly wide and deep subject of inkjet printing. The surface or substrate that you choose for your prints is incredibly important. It will determine the longevity of the print by the nature of the archival qualities that are inherent in the marriage of the ink and paper. Your choice will also affect presentation and framing choices.

Although you are faced with a multitude of choices concerning printing your digital images, we will add to that range of choices by explaining the textures that can be applied digitally in Photoshop. We can simulate canvas, watercolor paper, handmade papers, and more by using the patterns that are included in Photoshop.

I like to call Patterns a hidden Photoshop tool. Many long-time users of Photoshop have never ventured into the possibilities that await them when utilizing Patterns. Don't feel bad if it has escaped your notice. Folks tend to stumble into Patterns by accidentally selecting the Pattern Stamp tool, which is grouped with the Clone Stamp tool. Suddenly they are depositing a bubble pattern where they meant to use the current photograph. It probably doesn't help that when you view the options for the Pattern Stamp tool you discover weird and colorful patterns.

Seldom do photographers want to add a tie-dye or herringbone effect to their photos. And as for wrinkles, photographers are trying to get rid of them, not add them to their images. Accordingly, most folks turn away from the Pattern

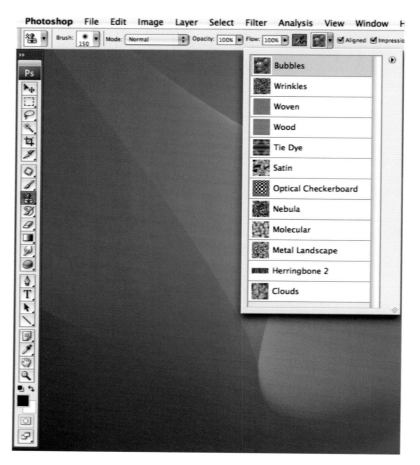

FIG. 2-41 Pattern Stamp tool options.

Stamp tool as quickly as they came and resolve to never touch it again. Few are the brave individuals who actually explore what lies behind that simple little triangle at the top of the list. As you know from your recent experience with the Brush Libraries, that little triangle indicates that there is more hidden from your view. If you actually click on that triangle, a new textural world will unfold for you.

Although you may access patterns through the use of the Pattern Stamp tool, it is recommended that you approach them through the Fill/Adjustment Layer icon at the bottom of the Layers Palette, sometimes referred to as the ying-yang symbol.

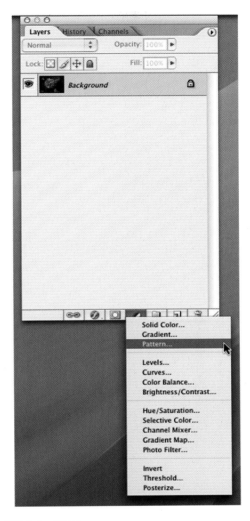

FIG. 2-42 Adding a Fill/Adjustment Layer.

The great advantage to applying your pattern fill using this method is the versatility that it gives. You can change your mind about which pattern to use. Once the Fill/Adjustment Layer is sitting above your image you can click on the pattern icon and change the pattern at will, very quickly.

You will notice that you can view the possible patterns by text alone, by small and large thumbnails, and by small and large lists. At the bottom of the menu are the Pattern Libraries already installed in Photoshop. The interface is almost identical to the one we saw for Brush Libraries.

FIG. 2-43 Selecting a pattern fill.

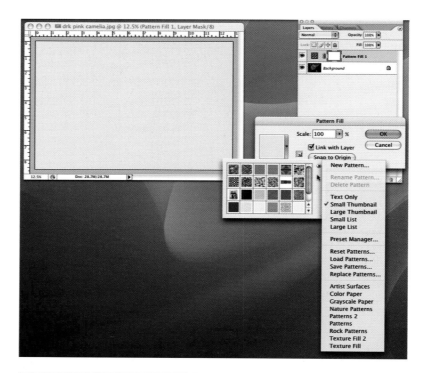

FIG. 2-44 Changing the scale of a pattern.

Patterns repeat, just as patterns repeat in nature, real paper, and fabric. With the Scale option, in the Pattern Fill menu, you can adjust the amount of repeat involved in your pattern. We often adjust the scale to 300–500%, when applying a texture on to our underlying image.

We've prepared a reference of all the stored Photoshop Patterns for you here. It will reduce your search time if you are looking for a specific pattern.

Artist Surfaces is a treasure trove of great paper and canvas surfaces.

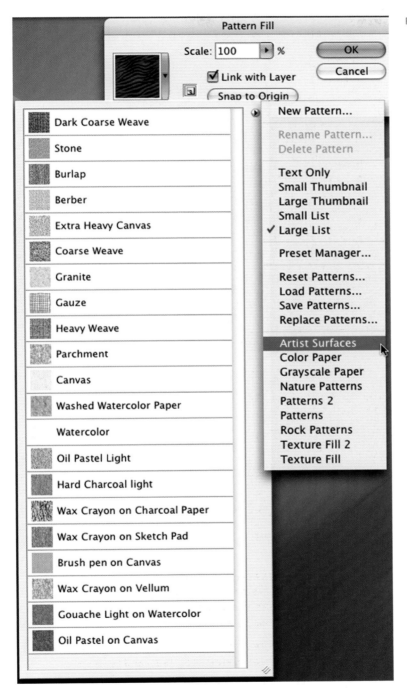

FIG. 2-45 Artist Surfaces.

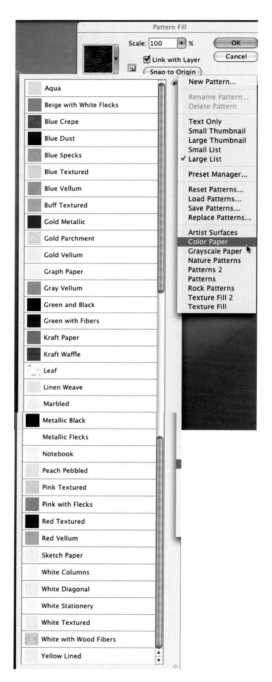

FIG. 2-46 Color Paper.

Although you may not wish to add color to your texture, some of the patterns in the Color Paper Library are quite nice. You can always desaturate a pattern to remove the color. Some of the examples in this library have good texture features that can be wonderful.

Grayscale Papers are great. We are particularly fond of the Fiber Papers.

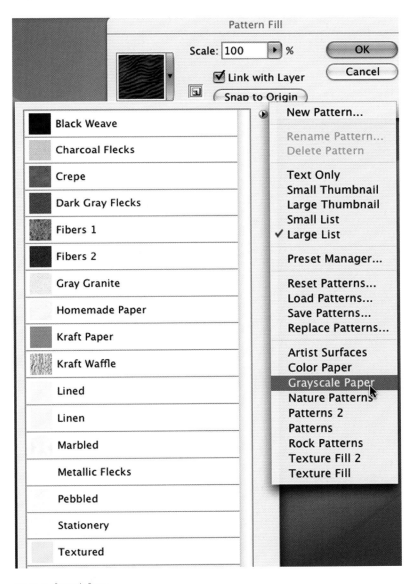

FIG. 2-47 Grayscale Paper.

Although Nature Patterns are not as likely to be of use to us with digital painting, don't totally discount them. The color can be desaturated, leaving the pattern behind.

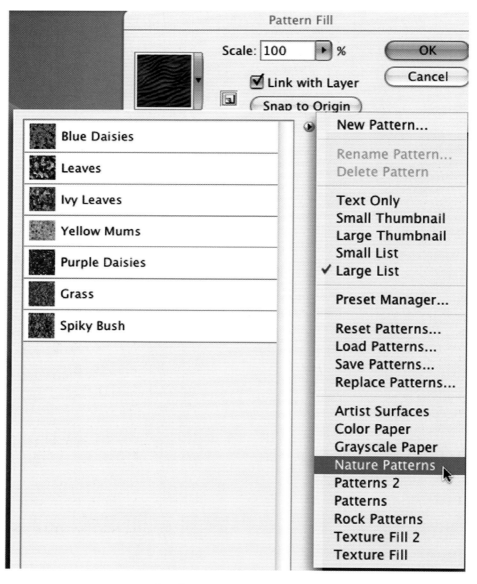

FIG. 2-48 Nature Patterns.

Favorites in this library include Coarse Weave and Stucco.

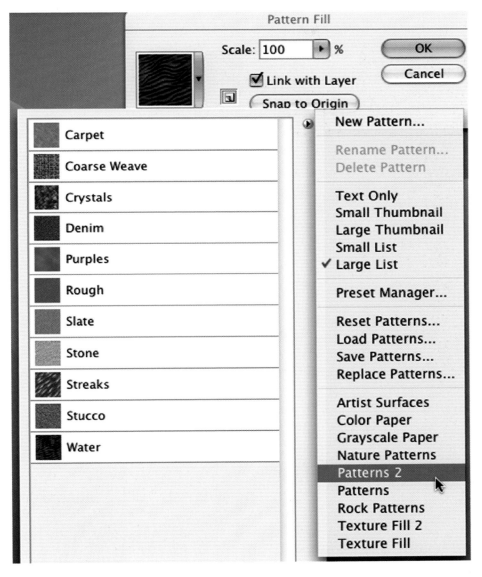

FIG. 2-49 Patterns 2.

Some of these patterns may work for your digital painting, but most are not conducive to giving a pattern that will be convincing.

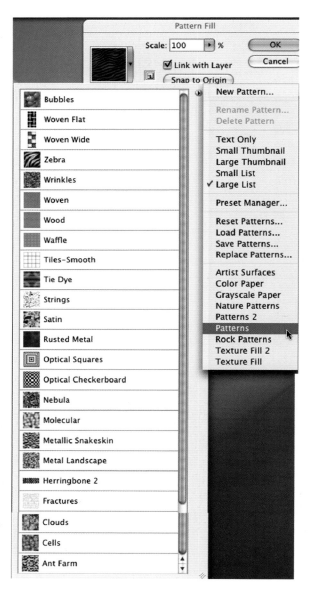

FIG. 2-50 Patterns.

Light Marble is the star in this Pattern Library.

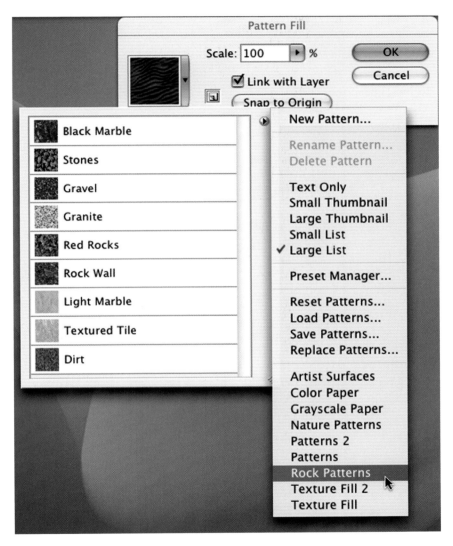

FIG. 2-51 Rock Patterns.

The textures and weaves are very effective patterns for digital painting.

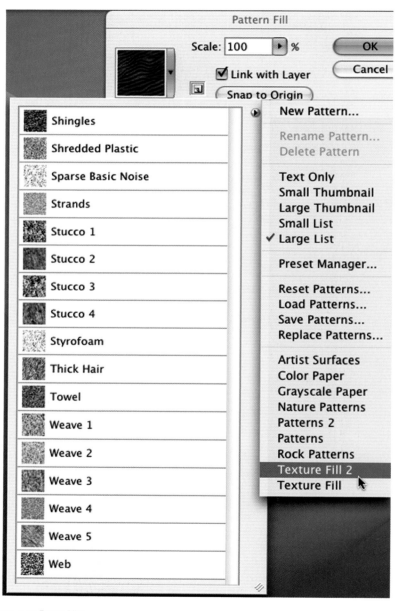

FIG. 2-52 Texture Fill 2.

Texture Fill is where you will find burlap and canvas. They are the superstars of this library.

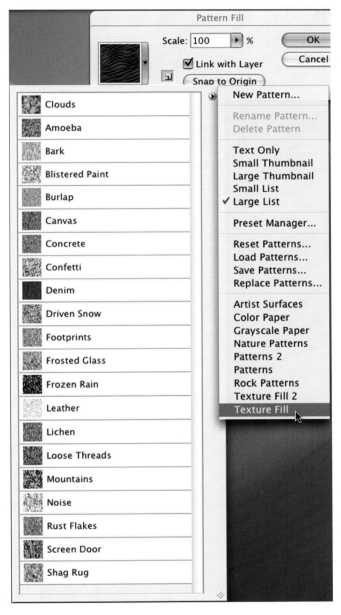

FIG. 2-53 Texture Fill.

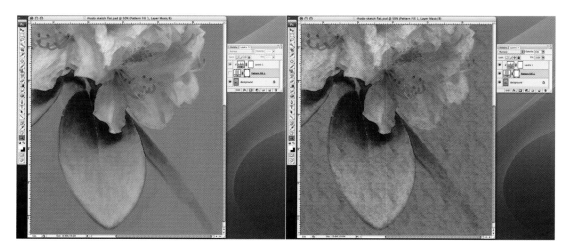

FIG. 2-54 Applying a Pattern Fill for textural effect.

You need to allow the image to show through the overlying pattern. Choose Multiply from the Blending Modes. The Multiply Blending Mode makes the color white disappear. Only areas with tone remain visible.

You may find that once the Pattern Fill is applied, the image seems too dark. Try lowering the opacity of the Pattern. Another tactic is to apply a Levels or Curves Adjustment Layer to lighten the pattern and/or image. On our example above, we lowered the opacity of the Pattern (Washed Watercolor Paper from the Artist's Surfaces Library) and lightened the pattern with a Levels Adjustment Layer that was confined to the Pattern Layer by means of a Clipping Mask.

Making Your Own Patterns

It is possible to make your own patterns and it is really quite easy.

FIG. 2-55 Leaves photo, leaves desaturated and lightened, and leaves blurred.

Practically anything can become a pattern. Our example is leaves on the ground in Pompeii. The file was 36 MB, which is too large for a pattern. The file was reduced in size to a 1.5 MB file and was desaturated and lightened. The photo was then blurred, using the Gaussian Blur Filter. The blurred pattern became a lumpy texture, not distinctly leaves. The choice to blur or not to blur is yours to make.

FIG. 2-56 Creating a pattern.

Once you have selected your pattern and altered it to suit your tastes, go to Edit – Define Pattern. Name the pattern. It will automatically appear in your pattern list for use.

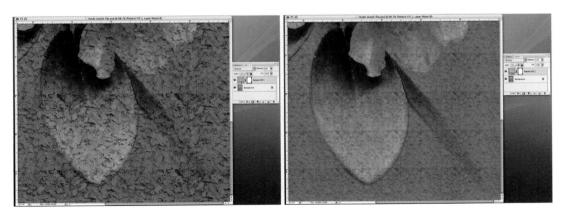

FIG. 2-57 Leaf Pattern applied and Blurred Leaf Pattern applied.

Think of all the possibilities! You could use a photograph of a bale of straw, a pile of rubber bands, sand at the beach, rusty metal, practically anything. You could also place a piece of white burlap or canvas on your scanner (a light color will work better than a darker one). All of these items can make a great pattern to use on your digital painting.

How to Apply a Pattern Texture

You may want to try out various pattern textures on your pastel drawing. For illustration purposes we will use a segment of a pastel drawing of a sunflower.

FIG. 2-58 The first step is to select Pattern from the options available in Adjustment Layers.

Don't be shocked by the existing default patterns that appear. We will probably not be using any of the default patterns.

Click on the triangular arrow, revealing the list of Pattern Libraries. The first one is called Artist Surfaces.

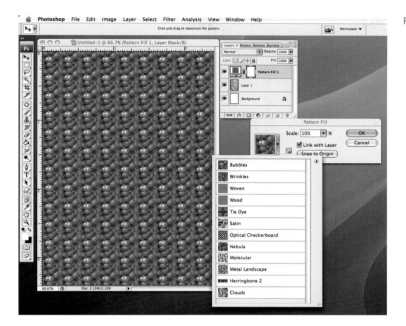

FIG. 2-59 Default patterns.

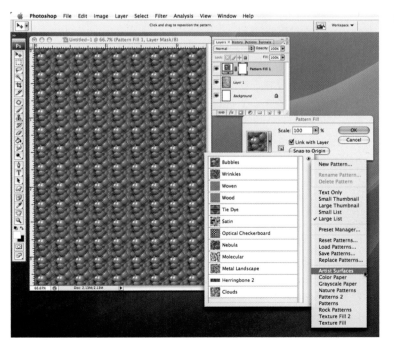

FIG. 2-60 Pattern Libraries.

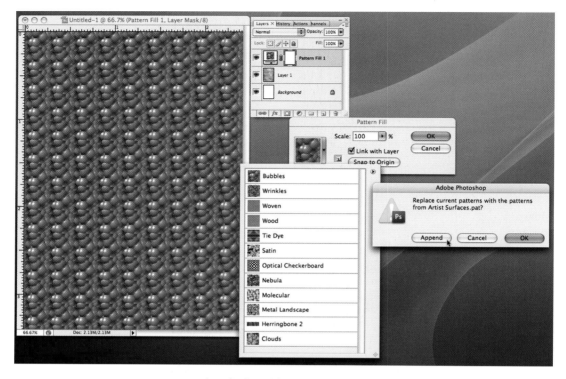

FIG. 2-61 Appending Pattern Libraries.

We can choose to replace the default library with our new library selection, or we can "append" it to the current list, increasing the list of current selections.

Hard Charcoal Light Pattern is selected from the Artist Surfaces Library. The scale remains set at the default of 100%.

To integrate this pattern, which is now obscuring the pastel beneath, we need to change the Blending Mode from Normal to Multiply. The Multiply Blending Mode makes the color white disappear.

The pattern that is selected will sometimes darken the drawing too much, or the effect will be too strong. To fix this, simply lower the opacity on the Pattern Adjustment Layer. The example shown here has an opacity of 73%.

Notice how the overall look of the drawing changes with the selection of the pattern.

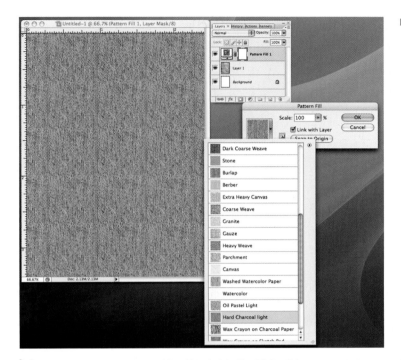

FIG. 2-62 Hard Charcoal Light Pattern.

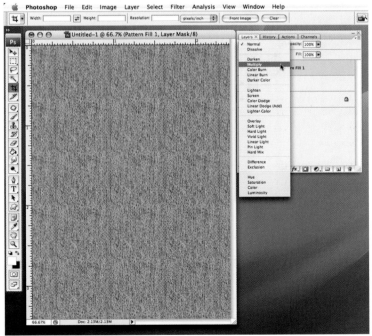

FIG. 2-63 Pattern Blending Mode change.

FIG. 2-64 Opacity change on the Pattern Adjustment Layer.

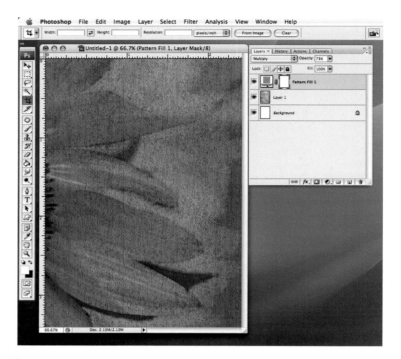

FIG. 2-65 Dark Coarse Weave from Artist Surfaces, set at 50% opacity.

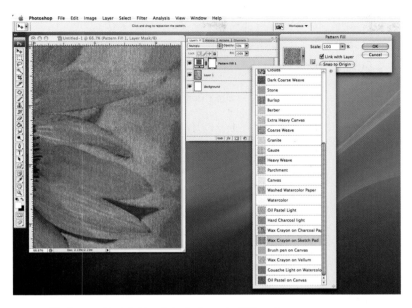

FIG. 2-66 Wax Crayon on Sketch Pad from Artists Surfaces, set at 50% opacity.

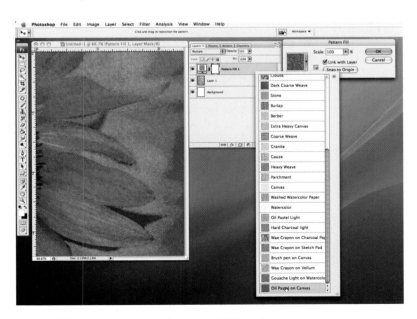

FIG. 2-67 Oil Pastel on Canvas from Artists Surfaces, set at 100% opacity.

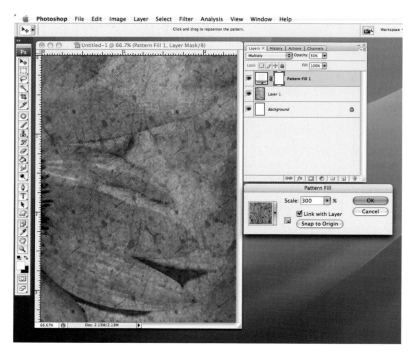

FIG. 2-68 Fibers 1 from Grayscale Paper, set at 50% opacity. Scale set at 300%.

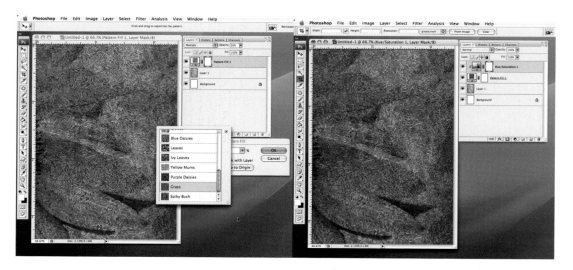

FIG. 2-69 Grass from Nature Patterns, set at 50% opacity. Scale set at 300%.

This pattern adds a green color. To remedy this color cast, add an Adjustment Layer of Hue and Saturation to desaturate the Grass Pattern.

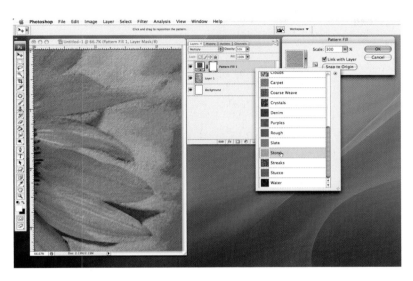

FIG. 2-70 Stone from Patterns 2, set at 50% opacity. Scale set at 300%.

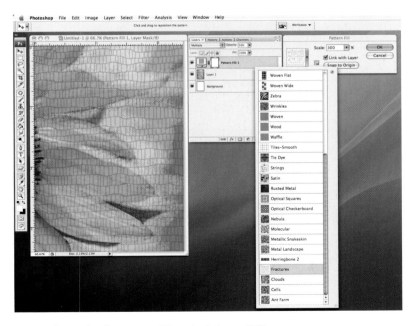

FIG. 2-71 Fractures from Patterns, set at 50% opacity. Scale set at 300%.

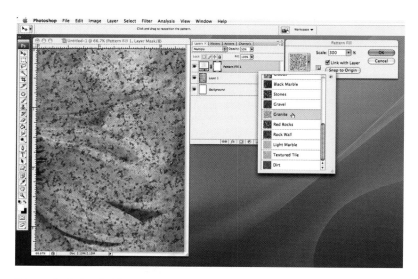

FIG. 2-72 Granite from Rock Patterns, set at 50% opacity. Scale set at 300%.

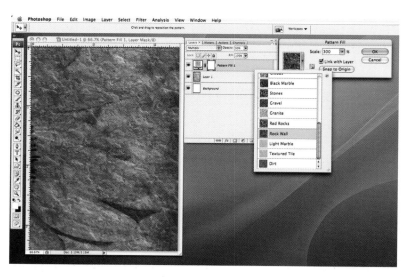

FIG. 2-73 Rock Wall from Rock Patterns, set at 50% opacity. Scale set at 300%.

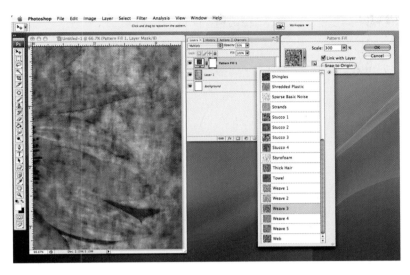

FIG. 2-74 Weave 3 from Texture Fill 2, set at 50% opacity. Scale set at 300%.

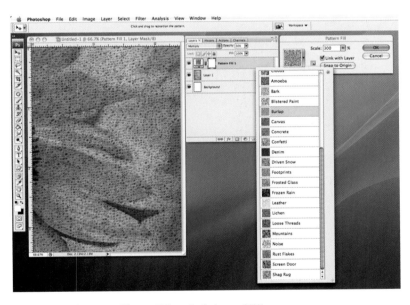

FIG. 2-75 Burlap from Texture Fill, set at 50% opacity. Scale set at 300%.

FIG. 2-76 Leather from Texture Fill, set at 50% opacity. Scale set at 300%.

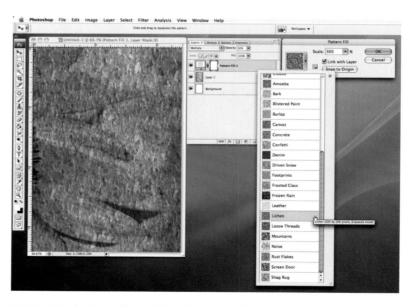

FIG. 2-77 Lichen from Texture Fill, set at 50% opacity. Scale set at 300%.

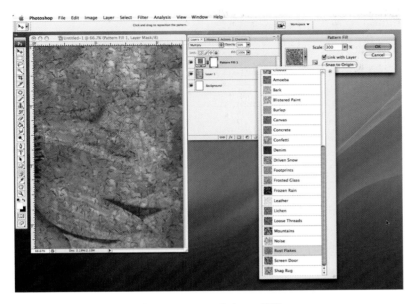

FIG. 2-78 Rust Flakes from Texture Fill, set at 50% opacity. Scale set at 300%.

These are just a few samplings of the myriad of textures and patterns that are available to apply to your artwork. Try them out. Make your own. Try varying the scale and the opacity. Many rewards await you in this world of texture.

The power of an arsenal of brushes of various sizes and textures, coupled with the ability to apply textures through the use of patterns, cannot be underestimated. These simple tools, at your fingertips, can greatly enhance your imagery and create wonderful painterly effects. These tools will be used for various effects throughout this book. I encourage you to experiment with them. Take them for a digital test drive!

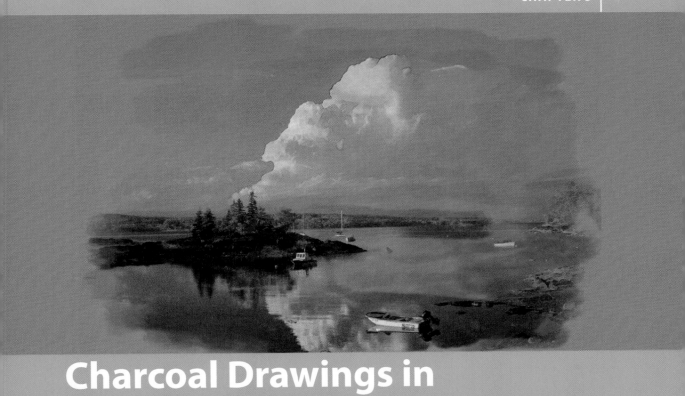

CHAPTER 3

Charcoal Drawings in Photoshop

Brief History of Charcoal

Charcoal drawings have been produced since early humans used burned twigs to draw on cave walls. It was and continues to be a great tool for making an expressive mark. Artists today continue in that tradition using real charcoal, compressed charcoal in pencils, and various conte pencils and chalks.

Some charcoal is derived from burned hardwood. Another type, frequently called vine charcoal, is made from tree twigs, like the willow. Bamboo is yet another source, used in the traditional Japanese Sumi-e. Modern charcoal production for art materials uses a binder of gum to compress the charcoal and create various degrees of hardness in the drawing implement.

Charcoal drawings are often made as preliminary first drafts of a painting. Charcoal is a very expressive medium that yields a mark that responds well to pressure. An accumulation of carbon dust is deposited on the paper or

FIG. 3-1 New England Cove.

canvas. Generally a fixative is sprayed on the drawing to minimize accidental smearing.

Michelangelo and Leonardo da Vinci were avid users of charcoal. In the tradition of these great masters, we humbly suggest that we can get similar effects using Photoshop. Our charcoal is going to be made up of pixels.

Since charcoal is a black-and-white medium, you might consider using some of your black-and-white photographs for this technique. If you choose a color image, it is, of course, easy to desaturate your photo, converting it to a black-and-white image.

Charcoal Techniques

FIG. 3-2 Original photograph of a Camellia flower.

Select a photograph that you would like to convert into a charcoal drawing. Correct any flaws on that photograph first, using tools like the Clone Stamp tool.

Add a new layer. Select a color for this layer. Select the layer and Edit – Fill with the color you have selected for your charcoal paper. This is like shopping in an art supply store, browsing through the drawers of various papers, looking for the exact shade of charcoal paper that you would like to use.

Copy the corrected background photo and place it on top of the stack of layers. On this new layer use Filters – Stylize – Glowing Edges Filter.

FIG. 3-3 Add a charcoal paper layer.

FIG. 3-4 Copy the Background Layer.

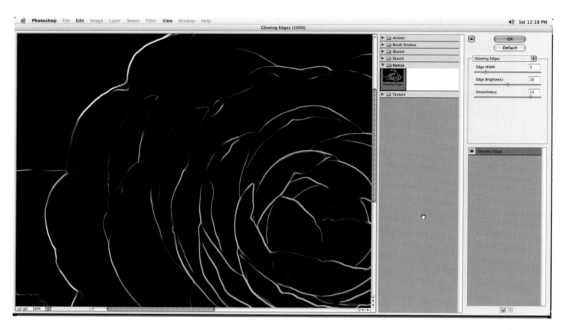

FIG. 3-5 Manipulate the Glowing Edges sliders.

Glowing Edges is one of those wacky filters that I couldn't find a practical use for until I realized that the neon line could be converted to white or black, creating a drawing effect. Violà! My perception of the filter and its possible artistic possibilities changed in an instant.

Most Photoshop users have tried Filters – Stylize – Find Edges as a method of achieving a line drawing. Although Find Edges does create a line drawing, as it looks for differences along the edge of items, it does not give you any sliders to manipulate the brightness and thickness of those liners. Glowing Edges, its digital cousin, gives you tools to control the quality of your lines. When using Glowing Edges we generally want the line to be narrow and bright, with increased smoothness.

The Glowing Edges filter produces a black background with a neon, multi-colored line drawing. Don't be dismayed; this is just the means to the desired end. Go to Image – Adjustments – Invert. That will convert the image to a white background. Next, use Image – Adjustments – Desaturate to create a black-and-white line drawing.

Now the fun really begins! Set the Blending Mode of that drawing layer to Multiply. With Multiply as a Blending Mode, white disappears. Now you have a drawing on your charcoal paper.

FIG. 3-6 Creating a line drawing.

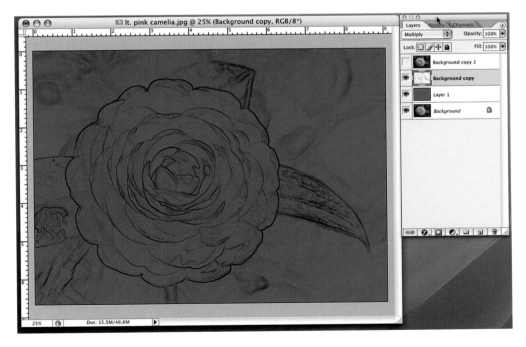

FIG. 3-7 Multiply Blending Mode.

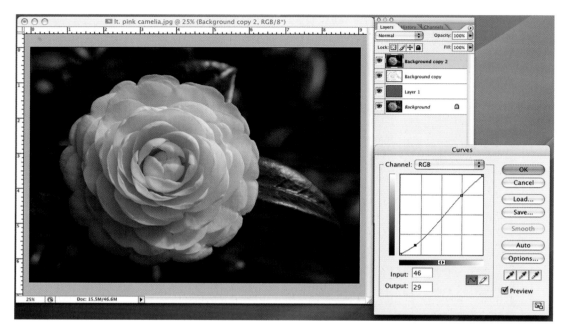

FIG. 3-8 New charcoal layer.

Copy the corrected background layer yet another time and place it at the top of your layer stack. Use Image – Adjustments – Desaturate, turning it into a black-and-white photo. Curves was used to increase the contrast of the image.

On this black-and-white photo layer go to Filter – Noise – Add Noise – Monochromatic and Gaussian. This will form your granular charcoal dust specks in the finished piece of artwork.

Staying on that top layer, go to Layer – Layer Masks – Hide All. That will immediately hide the current layer. Select a brush and paint with white on the mask, revealing those charcoal specks. One of our favorite brushes for this task is found in the Dry Media Brush Library and is called Charcoal Paper Brush.

We painted the flower area using white on the mask with that rough, textured brush. It yields a grainy, sketch-like effect due to the combination of the Add Noise filter and the textured brush that we are using.

Select the Paper Layer and go to Layer – New Fill Layer – Pattern and then click OK. This creates a Pattern Fill Adjustment Layer. There are so many varieties of textured patterns (see Chapter 2) to choose from. We chose the Charcoal Flecks Pattern, located in the Grayscale Paper Library. We increased the scale

FIG. 3-9   Making charcoal dust.

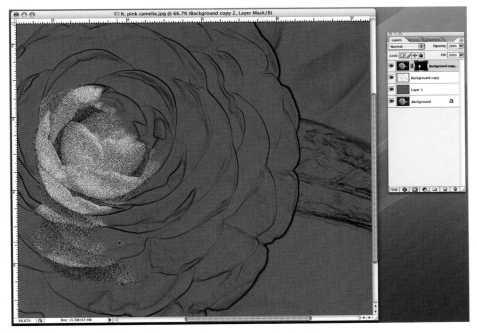

FIG. 3-10   Using a mask to "deposit" the charcoal dust specks.

FIG. 3-11 "Painting" on the charcoal specks.

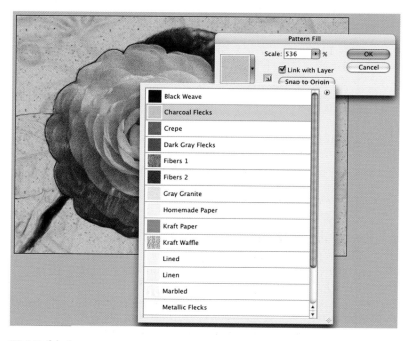

FIG. 3-12 Selecting a paper texture.

(or repeat of the pattern) to 536%. The Blending Mode for the Pattern Fill Adjustment Layer was set to Multiply.

FIG. 3-13 Saving the image for future changes.

It is always a wise choice to save your file with all the layers intact, in case you ever want to come back and make alterations. We generally save in the psd format (Photoshop Document). You can then flatten the document and use the Save As command. Using this method, you will not accidentally write over your layered original file. Another possibility is to use the Save and Copy option, in the Save As dialog.

Our next task is to create some sketchy edges for our image. The file was flattened and a new layer was created and filled with white (Edit – Fill – Choose White). We wanted this white layer to be underneath our image layer. Photoshop will not allow you to put a layer underneath a layer that is called Background. It is sort of like trying to put some building materials underneath the bedrock of the earth. If, however, the name of the layer is not Background, you will be okay. So simply change the name of the Background Layer. Double-click on the name Background, and type a new name in the menu box. This known as promoting a Background Layer to a Standard Layer. You can also drag the lock icon to the trash to promote.

FIG. 3-14 Making sketchy edges.

Add a Layer Mask to the Image Layer (Layer – Layer Mask – Reveal All). Paint on the mask with a rough, textured brush loaded with the color black. Do that all around the edges, revealing the pure white layer underneath.

Don't worry if you overdo it. A Layer Mask is totally forgiving. If you find you have gone too far, just switch to the color white on your mask to reverse any imperfections.

Duplicate this layer by dragging the layer to the new layer icon at the bottom of the Layer Palette. Set the Blending Mode to Multiply and reduce the opacity on this duplicate layer. We used 62% opacity. We continued to paint a bit more with black on the mask edges.

The charcoal Camellia seemed to have an antique quality to it, so to accent that feel a new layer was added and filled with a soft butterscotch color. The Blending Mode was set to Multiply and the opacity was lowered until the desired effect was achieved.

One of the best side effects of this technique is the absence of charcoal dust under your fingernails, the lack of dust smeared up your drawing arm, and no toxic fumes from fixative spray. Wouldn't Leonardo or Michelangelo be jealous?

FIG. 3-15 Antique effect.

Bridal Portrait with Tiny Charcoal Marks

A charcoal sketch effect can be very lovely for a portrait, especially a bridal portrait. Photographers are always looking for a different look for their portraits, for something that sets them apart from the competition. A charcoal sketch could be just that added something special.

In this example, a small brush size was used and many, many small strokes were crosshatched throughout the piece as it was made. There really is no substitute for tiny brush strokes for this effect. Take your time and render the piece section by section. Do not be tempted to use a large brush to cover more territory quickly. Slow and steady are the keys to this sketch effect.

The Pattern Texture used was Fibers 1 at 350% scale, from the Grayscale Pattern Library. The color of the paper was a soft golden-beige.

FIG. 3-16 Original bridal photograph.

FIG. 3-17   Portrait in progress.

FIG. 3-18 Completed bridal charcoal portrait.

Landscape Rendering with Smudgy Charcoal Look

In this example we will use a slightly different technique and arrive at a rendering that is more smudgy and soft. We will begin with a color digital shot of the Amalfi coast in Italy. The color of charcoal paper selected was a grayish-blue.

FIG. 3-19 Original photograph of Amalfi coastline.

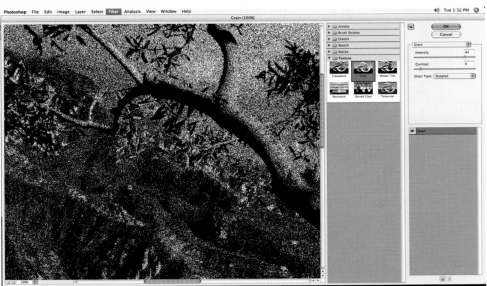

FIG. 3-20 Creating charcoal dust.

The charcoal dust is made differently this time, using Filter – Texture – Grain – Stippled, with black as our color. Using grain as our method of getting charcoal dust this time, we set the intensity at 84 and the contrast at 9. The preview gives a glimpse of the effect live.

FIG. 3-21   Rendering using a mask.

Using a Hide All Mask, we painted with white on the black mask using the Conte Pencil Brush preset from the Dry Media Brush Library. Vary the brush size as needed.

FIG. 3-22   Comparison between straight rendering and blurred, smudged effect.

The completed rendering seemed too sharp and crisp. The layers were flattened, the drawing layer was copied, and a Filter – Blur – Gaussian Blur was applied, softening the charcoal look on the duplicate layer. The desired appearance was somewhere between the two effects, so a mask was used and our rough brush was used at a low opacity (less than 20%) to pull some of the grain back through. This technique yields a softer look.

A nondestructive method of doing this is to eliminate flattening and convert to a Smart Object and apply a Smart Filter for Gaussian Blur. You can then change the blur values and blending modes and even mask the filter.

FIG. 3-23 Completed soft look charcoal drawing.

Conte and Charcoal Rendering

Another technique that can be used with charcoals is a neighboring art material, conte. Conte is a brownish-red chalk often used by charcoal artists in drawing, especially for portraits. Sometimes the artist will combine black charcoal, white chalk, and conte in a combined medium rendition.

In the real world, this type of drawing is extremely vulnerable to smudging and smearing due to the loose, chalky nature of the materials used. In our digital world we are free of smears. Our hands and nails are not covered in smeary dust particles. Mark that as another digital triumph over the real world.

Our next example, featuring a U.S. Civil War re-enactor on horseback, will make use of both the charcoal and the conte look.

FIG. 3-24 Original photograph of reenactor on horseback.

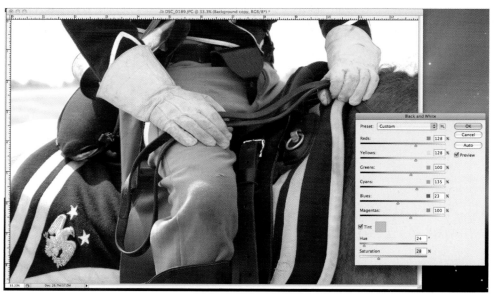

FIG. 3-25 Conte color is achieved in black-and-white conversion.

There are many techniques for achieving a sepia-type coloring for your photographs. In this example we duplicated the background layer and used the Image – Adjustment – Black-and-White Conversion, using a custom setting, modified from the high-contrast blue setting and checking the tint box, setting the Hue at 24 and Saturation at 28.

The Background Layer was duplicated again.

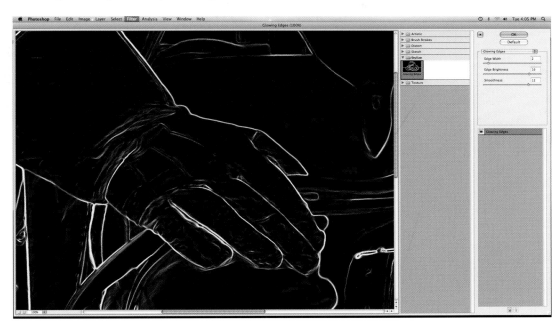

FIG. 3-26 Filter – Stylize – Glowing Edges for drawing effect.

The second duplicated Background Layer is used as a drawing layer. We used Filter – Stylize – Glowing Edges on it. The Edge Width was set to 2, the Edge Brightness was set at 10, and the Smoothness was set at 12. Once the filter was applied, the layer was desaturated and inverted under the Image – Invert command and Image – De-Saturate command.

A new layer was created and placed under the newly created drawing layer. It was filled with a soft beige tone, using Edit – Fill. That is our charcoal paper color.

The drawing layer was set to the Multiply Blending Mode. By setting the Blending Mode on Multiply, the color white disappears and we see our drawing on beige charcoal paper.

The background was duplicated again and a black-and-white conversion was made. Then Filter – Add Noise was used for a grainy effect, as we have seen in previous examples in this chapter.

Both the black-and-white layer and the conte layer had a Hide All Mask applied (Layer – Layer Mask – Hide All Mask). Both masks were painted with the color white at a low opacity (around 24%), building up both the conte

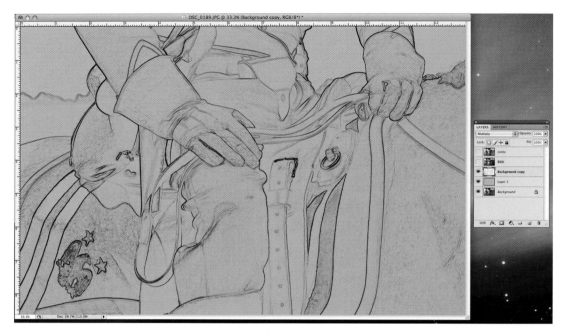

FIG. 3-27 Drawing effect using the Multiply Blending Mode.

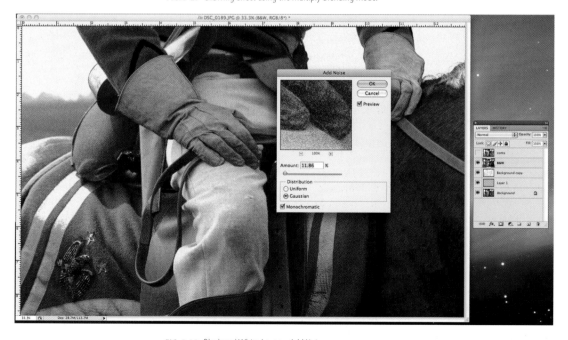

FIG. 3-28 Black and White Layer — Add Noise.

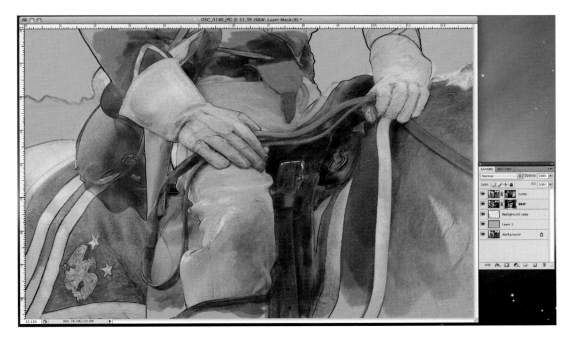

FIG. 3-29 Sketch with all layers intact.

brown color and the black-and-white colors. Some areas were left vacant to let the color of the paper show through.

With the drawing segment complete, a pattern was applied to the whole image, using Pattern Fill Layer. We selected Gray Granite as the pattern, set at 300% for scale. It is found in the Grayscale Paper Library under Patterns.

The Pattern Fill Layer was set to the Multiply Blending Mode.

As you can see, the possibilities are quite wide for charcoal interpretations within Photoshop. They can be strictly black-and-white or you can add a touch of color. We can approximate the grainy feel of charcoal by adding noise to our images. And last, we can add a paper texture to our sketch by means of a Pattern Fill Layer.

Something tells me that Leonardo would have jumped into this digital technology with both feet. As an artist, he was always experimenting with new materials. Sadly, that is the cause of the deterioration of his famed *The Last Supper*, in Milan. Leonardo was using oil paints on a water-based substrate, plaster. The two different materials have been fighting each other for almost six hundred years.

FIG. 3-30 Completed charcoal and conte sketch with pattern overlay.

Despite failures and setbacks, Leonardo continued to invent and dream. He certainly had insight, curiosity, and adventure in his spirit. That makes him a bona fide candidate for digital fine art in my mind.

We have a fabulous new material at our fingertips: pixels. And despite the use of digital charcoal, those very fingertips are clean. I invite you to explore and experiment, in the spirit of Leonardo da Vinci.

FIG. 3-31 Digital charcoal bird on flower.

CHAPTER 4

Pastel Drawing in Photoshop

Brief History of Pastels

In this chapter we are going to stir up some digital dust! When you think of pastels, do you conjure up the quick gestural work of ballet dancers by Degas? Did you know that Degas was also a fine photographer? Perhaps you think of the work of Toulouse-Lautrec. There is a long list of well-known artists who have worked in this medium.

Pastels are a fabulous art medium. They yield vivid colors. They are very immediate, allowing everything from a quick sketch to a more complex rendering. They are very portable. They do not require a solvent or medium, like oils and acrylics. They are dry, unlike watercolors, which require water to apply. They handle easily, like a pencil. In short, they are a great choice for making art.

Pastels are made from compressed particles of colored pigments. There are a riot of colors available. The pastel quality varies widely, from hard and

FIG. 4-1 Digital pastel of a Sicilian hill town.

economical versions for school children to soft, luscious, and expensive pastels for the serious artist. Of course, there are many types of pastels that lie somewhere in the middle of these two extremes, including the chalks that street artists use as they make their mini-masterpieces on the streets of tourist locales.

Although pastels are a dry media, in many ways they resemble a painting. They have the ability to create areas dense and rich in color. They can also be applied with a soft, delicate touch and a whisper of color.

Pastels work best on a paper that has texture, sometimes called a "tooth." In reality, the particles of chalk dust are "sawed" off the stick of chalk onto the textured paper. Some pastel artists use a special board or paper that has minute particles of sand embedded on the top. This sanded paper comes in many colors. In fact, most pastels are created on colored paper, not white paper.

It helps the computer artist to understand the look of a pastel as we try to create a similar feel with our computer generated art. Texture will be the key to the look and feel of traditional pastels. Fortunately, Photoshop is loaded with great tools and patterns to aid us in this task.

As a digital artist working in Photoshop, you will need to simulate the effect of colored particles of pigment on a textured surface. To accomplish this effect, our two main tools will be specialized brushes and textured papers. Brushes and textured paper are covered in Chapter 2.

Pastel Techniques

In this example we will start with the look of a basic pencil sketch, not unlike the preparation of a traditional pastel drawing. The photo used is actually a scan of a flower, which was placed directly on the scanning bed. Your scanner can make a great camera, with a shallow depth of field.

Duplicate your background layer and use Filter – Stylize – Glowing Edges on it. On that duplicate layer use Image – Adjustment – Invert.

This creates our sketch, but we still need to get rid of the color in this duplicate layer, so use Image – Adjustment – Desaturate. Now we have something that resembles a graphite pencil sketch.

Add a new layer above your Background Layer and fill it with the color that you would like for your paper. This is like selecting the pastel paper in the art supply store. I chose a light olive green. The next step is to set the drawing layer's Blending Mode to Multiply. This eliminates the color white, and the sketch appears on the colored paper.

FIG. 4-2 Original flower scan.

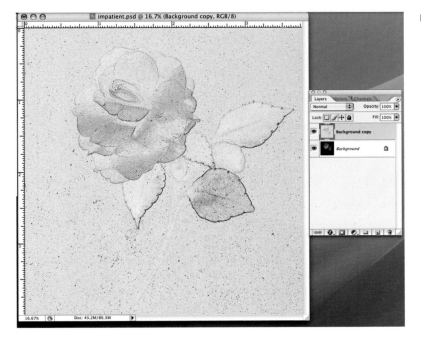

FIG. 4-3 Glowing Edges Filter applied.

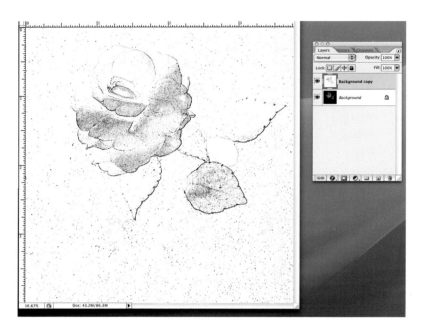

FIG. 4-4 Our pencil sketch.

FIG. 4-5 Sketch on pastel paper.

FIG. 4-6 Pastel sketch starts to emerge.

Duplicate the background layer again and add a Hide All Layer Mask (this is solidly black, revealing the sketch underneath). Select a very scratchy, irregular brush that reacts with a grainy feel. This can be found in your Brush Libraries, like Dry Media Brushes. Paint with the color white on this mask, using the grainy brush. It will pull the color from the photo and use it as pigment to be deposited on your sketch. Allow some paper to show through, as it would in a real pastel.

Now we will add a little more texture. Use a Pattern Fill Layer. Select a textured pattern for the surface texture of your paper. I usually enlarge the scale to 300–500%. I used the Charcoal Flecks Pattern. Set the Blending Mode for this adjustment layer to Multiply.

Note: I often add color and erase color on the mask several times, using that scruffy brush, to build up texture and enrich the quality of my mark making. If I want to further enhance the image, I may add another layer and paint with any color on that separate layer (which is above the nearly completed drawing, but beneath the Pattern Adjustment Layer. I often add a touch of a more saturated version of the color beneath, spicing up the general appearance.

FIG. 4-7 Adding a textured paper.

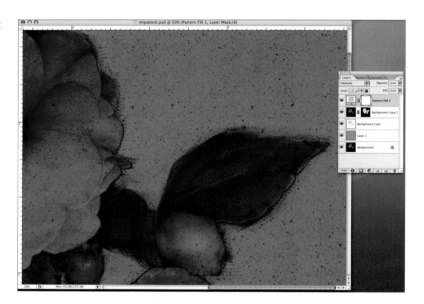

FIG. 4-8 Completed pastel sketch.

This example allows the sketch layer to softly lead the viewer into the image. This effect was achieved by not extending the colored pastels layer all the way to the edges. This gradual method of leading the viewer's eye into the center of the image is a good design component. An additional component on this

FIG. 4-9 Venetian canal.

depiction of a Venetian canal is the application of a paper texture on top, using the patterns available in Photoshop.

Making a Pastel Brush

There are many different types of brushes available to you in Photoshop in various libraries (see Chapter 2). There are several that work very well as a pastel brush. These brushes have areas, within the stroke, that are free of color. The brush "skips" over some areas. This simulates real-world pastels and textured paper or board. But, if you are a stickler for authenticity, we can make our own pastel brush.

FIG. 4-10   Photo of real pastel application.

We made a few marks on a sanded pastel board that was medium in tone. The pastel colors used were white and a dark brown. I scanned the marks into my computer. Notice the areas of the stroke that are skipped and the rough edges of the stroke.

Since the marks were in color, the image was desaturated (Image – Adjustments – Desaturate).

The grey sanded board needed to become white for this technique, so the tones were adjusted in Curves. Since the bumpy, sand-covered board still showed some texture in the areas outside the mark, those white areas were painted with a brush loaded with white.

All that is needed to create a new brush from this doctored scan is to go to Edit – Define Brush Preset.

The next step is simple—name your new brush. This one is huge (over 600 pixels wide), but brushes can always be scaled down.

The next time you pull down the brush selection list, you will notice your new brush at the end of the brush option list.

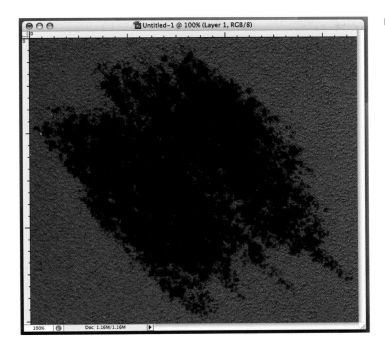

FIG. 4-11 Desaturated scan.

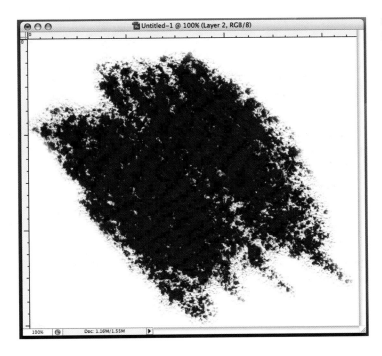

FIG. 4-12 Dark pastel mark on white board.

FIG. 4-13   Define Brush Preset.

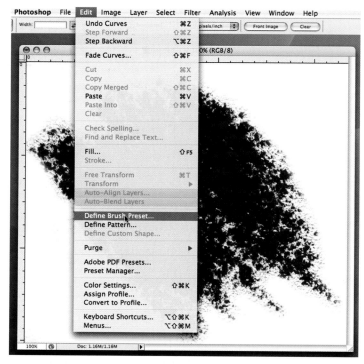

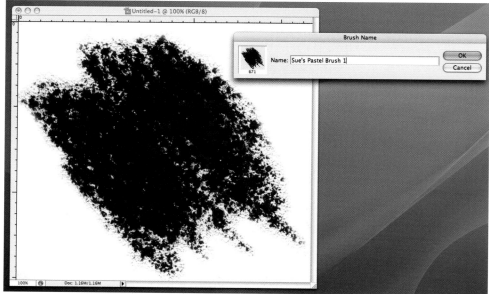

FIG. 4-14   Name your new brush.

FIG. 4-15 Your brush is added to the brush list.

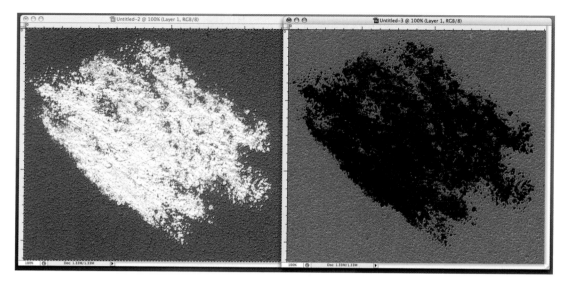

FIG. 4-16 Another brush made – Desaturate and Invert.

The other scanned pastel mark was made with white pastel. Again, desaturate the color. The image was then inverted (Image – Adjustments – Invert). After the tones were modified in Curves, making the gray areas white, the brush was defined as another brush preset. The possibilities are virtually endless; you can make as many custom brushes as you want.

Now we can try that new brush.

This pastel of newborn baby Anne followed all the steps that we used in our first example (Figures 4-2 to 4-8). The entire piece was executed with our new custom brush, Sue's Pastel Brush #1. We varied the size of the brush as needed.

Feel free to add another layer and brush on additional color to accent the composition. Because the additional color is confined to a separate layer, it can easily be erased or removed without harming the original sketch.

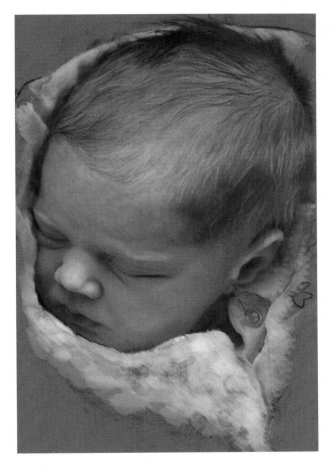

FIG. 4-17 Pastel of baby Anne.

Printing Considerations

There are so many quality papers now available for digital printing. We recommend using a textured paper from a good paper mill, a paper that has a bit of a bump in the surface. It will continue to enhance the feel of your digital pastel.

Be brave. Add another blank layer, and using a scratchy brush (perhaps of your own design) add additional colors. Usually these complimentary strokes should be done at a low opacity. Experiment. Have fun stirring up some digital dust!

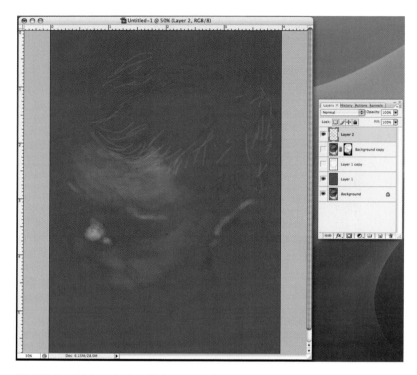

FIG. 4-18 Accent strokes and colors added on a separate layer.

FIG. 4-19 White peony digital pastel rendering.

FIG. 4-20 Pastel rendering of a Rhododendron.

FIG. 4-21 Digital pastel of Capri Lane.

CHAPTER 5

Painting with Watercolors in Photoshop

M ost of us think of Photoshop as a software program devoted solely to photo enhancement. We use Photoshop to alter the crop on our image, enhance saturation or contrast, remove unsightly blemishes or red eye, and, in short, improve our photographs. Yes, Photoshop is indeed the premiere program for these tasks. But have you ever thought about painting in Photoshop? I don't mean running your image through the Watercolor Filter, expecting a watercolor painting to emerge in seconds. I mean making brush strokes that are truly painterly.

Photoshop contains hidden tools that are perfect for painting. Like many hidden things, they are actually right there in plain view. It is like the experience of shopping for a particular make of car. Once you begin concentrating on that type of car, you suddenly see them everywhere you travel. The truth, of course, is that the number of those cars hasn't changed; you just weren't looking for

FIG. 5-1 Orchid.

that make before. Likewise, once you start to concentrate on the tool options for painting, you will see that they are plentiful. You just didn't notice them before.

You undoubtedly use the Brush tool in Photoshop, probably for masking and other tasks. I'll hazard a guess that you use various sizes of the traditional Hard Edge and Soft Edge Brush. They are the most frequently used and practical Brush tools. Have you ever allowed yourself to look for any other type of Photoshop brush? Have you made a brush of your own from scratch? Most folks will answer "no." If you haven't yet read Chapter 2, devoted to all the brushes and papers available, you probably want to take a good look there now.

Brief History of Watercolor

Watercolor is a fabulous art medium. It can be used to create a fresh, quick, and semitransparent painting. It can be used in the field, "plein air," as the enthusiasts call it. It can be layered with washes, building up the density of color, creating a densely colored painting. Watercolor paintings can be quick or labored in the amount of time required. The look varies, depending on intent and the techniques used.

Art supply stores sell watercolors in dry cakes or in tubes filled with wet paint. As the name implies, the medium is reconstituted or thinned with water. There is a bit of binder used in watercolors (usually gum arabic, with glycerin). Another type of watercolor is gouache. Gouache is more opaque due to opacifiers, like chalk or zinc oxide. More opaque than gouache is tempera. Tempera pigments can be mixed with an egg yolk as a binder. Andrew Wyeth is a modern master of egg tempera painting. As you can see, there are many water media paints available.

One popular technique is called wet-on-wet. The watercolor paper is taped down onto a drawing board, and a wash of water is applied with a wide, flat brush. The water is allowed to absorb and evaporate a bit. Watercolor washes are then applied, thus working wet paint into wet paper. This technique is often used for the sky area of landscape paintings. When working wet-on-wet, pigment rapidly spreads out in the wet surface, fanning color into wet areas.

The opposite effect is called dry brush. In this technique, paint is dabbed off the brush onto an absorbent toweling or cloth, leaving a very minimal amount of paint on the brush. That thin pigment is then applied in an almost dry manner. This technique is good for hair, foliage, etc.

Watercolor paper is often thick, even very thick. It is sold by the sheet or in a "block." A block is a stack of sheets, bound together along the outside edges. Watercolor paper often has a very noticeable texture and is white or off-white in color. Many watercolorists do not use a white pigment, allowing the white of the paper to shine through where needed. Avoiding future white areas of the painting, as you paint can take some very careful planning.

Some artists believe that the medium of watercolors is one of the most difficult to master. We will simulate watercolor mediums digitally in this chapter.

Watercolor Technique

FIG. 5-2 Photograph of Icelandic scene.

Begin by opening a photograph that you would like to render in a watercolor painting effect. My photograph was taken in Iceland, near dusk. Duplicate the photo twice. (Note: An easy method to duplicate a layer is to drag the layer to the New Layer icon, at the bottom of the Layers Palette.)

On the first duplicate layer, directly above the background image, apply Filter – Blur – Smart Blur. This lessens detail, creating blocks of color. On the second duplicate layer, on top of the layer stack, apply Filter – Stylize – Glowing Edges. Proceed, on that same layer, to use Layer – Adjustments – Invert and then Layers – Adjustments – Desaturate. That creates a pencil-like drawing. Choose Multiply as the Blending Mode and use an opacity of about 50%.

Now, duplicate the original photo again, for the third time. Place it on the top of the layer stack. Use Image – Adjustments – Invert on this layer and set the Blending Mode to Color Dodge. This will be our canvas.

Select the Dry Brush from the Natural Brush 2 Collection. Paint with black, at a low opacity, on the top layer. This will start "roughing-in" our watercolor painting. Let some white show through, especially along the outside edges.

FIG. 5-3 Beginning layers.

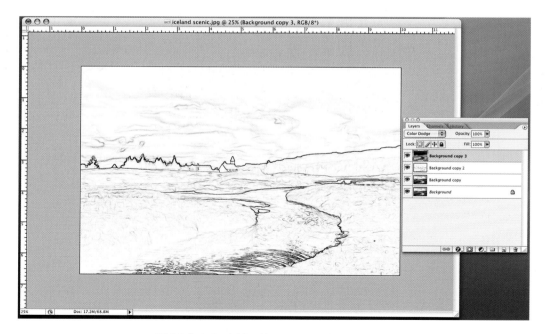

FIG. 5-4 Beginning sketch and layers.

It may seem quite weird to be painting with black on the color dodge layer but it really works!

Switch to the Wet Media Brushes and select Watercolor Texture Surface Brush Preset. Vary the size and opacity and stroke on some detail.

FIG. 5-5 Pattern texture applied.

Select Pattern in the Layer Adjustments. Here is where our paper textures come in. I used Watercolor at 200% scale. I set the Blending Mode to Multiply at 70% opacity. That lends the textural feel of watercolor paper. (Instructions on using Pattern textures can be found in Chapter 2).

The next step is not necessary, but it adds a little detail. Duplicate the original photo yet again. I put it on the top of the layer stack and applied the Watercolor Filter to it. Remember early in this book I said that putting a Watercolor Filter on a photo does not make it a watercolor. I stand by that statement, but here is where it can be useful.

FIG. 5-6 Adding detail.

Add a Hide All Layer Mask. That conceals the new, watercolor-filtered layer. Paint on the mask with white, at a low opacity, revealing little glimpses of that watercolor effect in random areas. This adds just the tiniest bit of that effect. It is like the cherry on the top of an ice cream sundae.

Finally, I removed the outline sketch for a more subtle, cohesive appearance. It was the underlying "bones" or sketch for the subsequent painting, and is no longer needed. This piece, and others similar in effect, look good when they are printed on a good quality, bumpy, inkjet watercolor paper.

Watercolor Brushes

When simulating the effect of a true watercolor it is important to pick the correct brush for the desired effect. There are many options contained in Photoshop. It would be wise to experiment on a sample image, just to get the feel of the various brushes.

Here are some examples. In all cases the opacity was set to 30%.

FIG. 5-7 Completed watercolor.

FIG. 5-8 Watercolor Light Opacity Brush from the Wet Media Brushes.

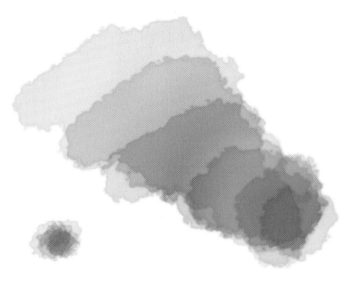

FIG. 5-9 Watercolor Textured Surface Brush from the Wet Media Brushes.

FIG. 5-10 Watercolor Fat Tip Brush from the Wet Media Brushes.

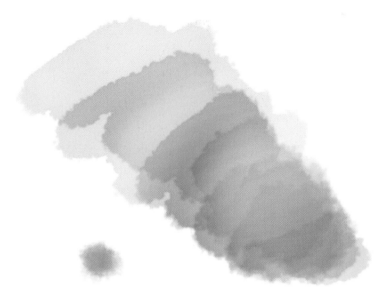

FIG. 5-11 Watercolor Heavy Medium Tip Brush from the Wet Media Brushes.

FIG. 5-12 Watercolor Heavy Loaded Brush from the Wet Media Brushes.

117

FIG. 5-13 Brush Light Texture Medium Tip from the Wet Media Brushes.

Pattern Stamp Watercolor Technique

Photoshop has so many ways in which we can make a painting. The technique in this tutorial uses a tool that you may have never used before: the Pattern Stamp tool.

I find that most Photoshop users only stumble upon the Pattern Stamp tool when they reach for the Clone Stamp tool and accidentally grab the Pattern Stamp tool, since it is bundled with the Clone Stamp tool. They realize their mistake when a bizarre pattern of bubbles is deposited on their photo. The Bubble Pattern is the default pattern.

We will use this underutilized tool to create a painting. This technique is easy, quick, and fun.

First select a photograph that is suitable for a painting. I selected a photo of a gull, taken in Maine.

FIG. 5-14 Original photo of seagull.

FIG. 5-15 New pattern created.

Use Select – All. Chose Edit – Define Pattern. The photo will appear in the dialogue box, with a suggested name. Click on OK.

FIG. 5-16 New pattern added to the pattern list.

Select the Pattern Stamp tool. At the top of the page, where all the modifiers appear for your tools, scroll down through the list of the patterns and you will discover your photo at the bottom of the list. It is now officially a pattern.

FIG. 5-17 Add a new layer and fill with white.

Add a new layer and fill it with the color white (Edit – Fill).

FIG. 5-18 Rough underpainting.

With the Pattern Stamp tool selected, choose a brush. I used the Watercolor Heavy Pigments Brush, from the Wet Media Library of brushes. Brush libraries are located in a pull-down menu when you click on the triangle at the top right-hand side of the Brush menu. With a large version of that brush, I roughed in the painting on the white layer. Be sure to have the Impressionist option checked in the Options bar.

FIG. 5-19 Smaller brush creates more detail.

I then switched to another Wet Media Brush, the Watercolor Heavy Medium Tip Brush, and used a small brush to start to add more exact placement of colors.

FIG. 5-20 Close-up of added detail.

Continue brushing the surface of the painting, trying to follow the contour of the objects that you are painting. Vary the size of the brush as needed. A smaller brush will yield more detail.

FIG. 5-21 Accent colors added.

Since we are painting, why not add a little accent color to the sky? Add a new transparent layer. On that layer some additional blue and pink were added with a large brush at a low opacity.

FIG. 5-22 Blur the watercolor additions to the sky.

To add to the effect of a watercolor, I used the Blur – Motion Blur Filter. The direction of the blur was set to be vertical to the painting, thus creating a wash of color that blended and ran a bit with our digital gravity, just like a real watercolor.

FIG. 5-23 Check for flaws.

It is always wise to go back into the painting and refine it in areas. I recommend that you inspect the entire painting, section by section, making alterations as you find the need.

FIG. 5-24 Completed painting.

This is the completed watercolor painting made with the Pattern Stamp tool.

I hope you enjoy this simple painting technique. In reality, the Pattern Stamp tool used your entire original photo as the clone source, duplicating the colors and placement of those colors. You determine the painterly effect by your choice of a particular brush. Remember that a smaller brush creates more detail. A larger brush is good for roughing-in the basic painting, or for a loose rendition. Go crazy with this artistic technique. Vary your brushes for different effects and see where this process takes your photos.

Here is another example of digital watercolor paintings made with this Pattern Stamp tool technique.

Art History Brush Watercolor Technique

The Art History Brush, bundled with the History Brush, is a wacky brush. Its icon has a curly-Q stroke on the brush. That is your first clue about the nature of this brush. It deposits marks that have names such as tight curl, loose medium, dab, and tight short. It pulls color information from the photo you opened. In essence, it is using the photo as your clone source and depositing a particular looking brush stroke on another layer.

FIG. 5-25 Capri rowboat made with Pattern Stamp tool.

For our example here, we are going to use the dab brush stroke, which resembles pointillism, a style of art popularized by Georges-Pierre Seurat, in the neo-impressionism era of painting.

FIG. 5-26 Original photograph of daffodil still life.

After studying the original photograph, we decided to change the background.

FIG. 5-27 A new background was added.

A new layer was added and the Gradient tool (solid color to transparent) was applied to the new layer. That provided a smooth, uniform transition of color.

FIG. 5-28 Layer Mask is used to reclaim the vase and flowers.

A Layer Mask was added. You can get a layer mask from Layer – Layer Mask or by clicking on the Layer Mask icon at the bottom of the Layers Palette. Paint, on the mask, with black to reveal the vase and flowers. If you make a mistake, just switch to the color white. It is totally nondestructive to the image and very forgiving of any mistakes. Flatten the layers.

FIG. 5-29 Select the Art History Brush tool.

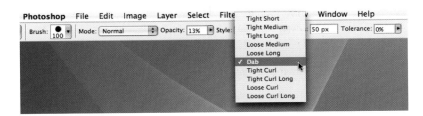

FIG. 5-30 Select the dab stroke.

Try out all the brushes—they are unusual. Some resemble wavy strings, others lint from your clothes dryer.

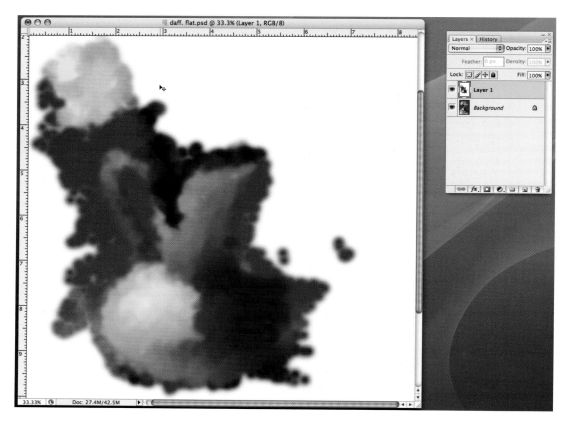

FIG. 5-31 Dab strokes are applied.

Select a brush and determine the diameter of the brush. We used the Watercolor Fat Tip brush from the Wet Media Library of brushes. Start to apply the dabs. A big brush yields a large, soft area of color. A smaller brush yields a smaller sampling and more detail.

FIG. 5-32 The underpainting of dab strokes is complete.

FIG. 5-33 Motion blur is applied to the painting layer.

To achieve the wet, blurry, drippy feel of a watercolor we applied a filter: Blur – Motion Blur. The angle was set to 90 degrees to simulate the effects of gravity.

We returned to the Art History Brush and applied more strokes. We used a smaller brush at a low opacity, finessing the strokes onto the painting. The same Watercolor Fat Tip Brush was used.

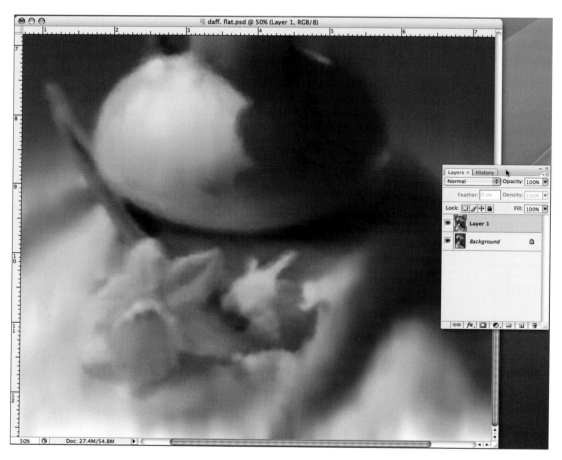

FIG. 5-34 Refining the image—close-up.

A new layer was added and additional accent colors were painted on that layer. This is our painting and we can choose to enhance the painting further. To that end, a new layer was added and colors were selected and painted onto that separate layer.

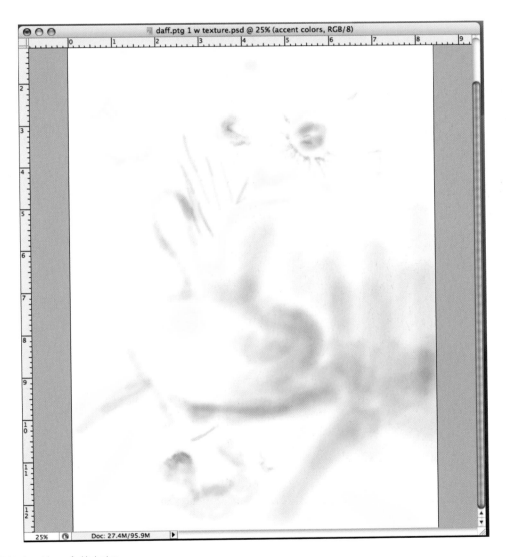

FIG. 5-35 Accent layer of added colors.

FIG. 5-36 Completed watercolor painting made with the Art History Brush technique.

Not every photograph will be a good candidate for a watercolor. I look for an image that would benefit from a more subdued color saturation rendering. Opacity plays a big part. I like to let some of the white watercolor paper show around the edges. A real watercolor is often built layer by layer, increasing opacity in specific areas. The paint often fades out into the white paper. If you choose to work in this vein, remember that the blank white areas will be a big part of your composition. Make them work for you.

Simple Two-Layer Watercolor Painting

The following technique is very simple and only requires two layers. It relies on the Pattern Stamp tool and expressive brushes. Pick a simple photograph that is free of clutter and a lot of unnecessary detail. Keep it simple.

FIG. 5-37 Original photograph of a Dall sheep on a hilltop in Alaska.

This photograph lent itself to a watercolor rendition. A loose pale background was a nice way to render the mountainside. A bit of detail, but not too much, would be a good way to render the sheep.

Select the entire image and go to Edit – Define Pattern. The photo will appear. Name it, creating a pattern source from which we will draw later. Add another layer and Edit – Fill with the color white.

Most paintings begin in a loose manner. Color areas are blocked into place. Our loose, first step used the Pattern Stamp tool (grouped with the Clone Stamp tool). The brush selected, the Spray Brush 68, came from the Natural

FIG. 5-38 Creating a Pattern Stamp.

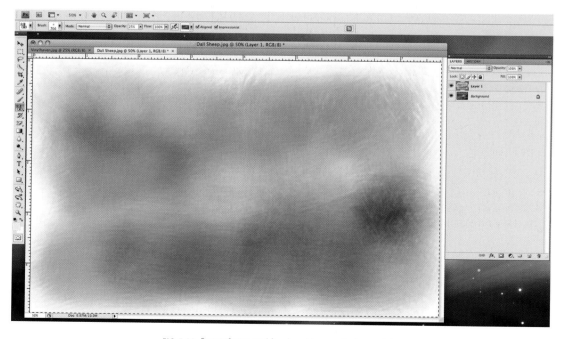

FIG. 5-39 Pattern Stamp used for a broad, loose preliminary painting.

Brushes Library. It was enlarged to 700 pixels in diameter. The opacity of the brush was set to 25%. A light application of paint was dabbed on the white layer. Again, be sure that the Impressionist box is checked.

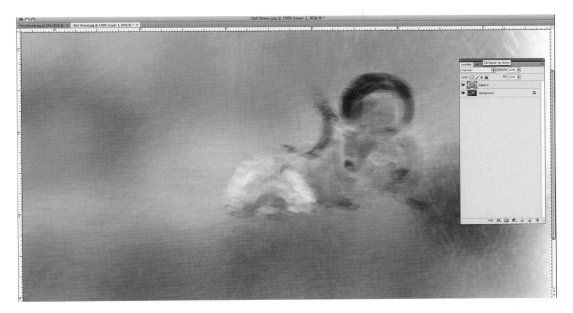

FIG. 5-40 The Dall sheep was roughed in with the Watercolor Loaded Wet Flat Brush.

The next step was performed with a different brush tip, still using the Pattern Stamp Brush. That tool is pulling the color and placement information from the original photograph, because we defined the whole photo as the source pattern. The next brush is the Watercolor Loaded Wet Flat Tip Brush from the default Brush Library. Using a smaller diameter brush at a low opacity (approximately 20–25%), the sheep was lightly articulated.

A Reveal All Mask was added to the painted layer (Layer – Layer Mask – Reveal All Layer Mask, or click on the Mask icon at the bottom of the Layer Palette). Gently paint a light opacity of black (about 10%) on the mask, revealing a touch of the photograph on the layer beneath.

FIG. 5-41 Bringing in photographic detail with a mask.

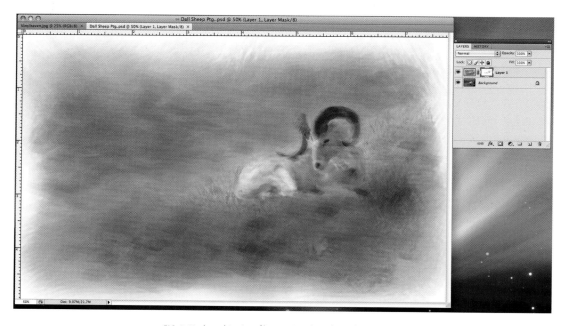

FIG. 5-42 A combination of loose, painterly strokes and a tiny bit of detail.

This painting technique only requires two layers and a single Layer Mask to render a watercolor painting. Again, the keys to this process are a light opacity of the brush and selection of appropriate brushes.

FIG. 5-43 Close-up of minimal detail.

Remember to keep it simple. Work lightly. A watercolor has a sense of transparency. That is our goal in achieving a digital watercolor. This technique is similar to the one used on our earlier seagull. No accent colors or Pattern Texture Adjustment Layer were added to the sheep painting.

You can create your own combination of techniques to create a watercolor, always keeping in mind the nature of a true watercolor. Watercolors are luminously transparent, with a build-up of colors from many layered applications. Details and opacity appear in selected areas of the painting. Try to keep it loose and free. Avoid too much detail. Above all, have fun with your painting techniques.

FIG. 5-44 Watercolor of Maine lighthouse.

CHAPTER 6

Painting with Oil Paints in Photoshop

Brief History of Oil Painting

Oil painting is perhaps the most revered of all classic painting techniques. Museums are full of oil paintings that have survived many centuries. Paintings of this type can endure "cleanings" by restoration experts, as the need arises. The same cannot be said for pastels or watercolors.

Traditionally the dry pigments are mixed with oils. The oils can be derived from seeds, as with linseed oil, and are sometimes boiled with tree resins. The variety of "mediums" is vast and can include the addition of waxes. The finish of the painting can be high gloss or matte depending on the medium used.

Oil paintings can be applied to wooden panels or canvas, stretched on a wooden framework. The support for the painting is prepared in advance of the actual painting process, with a material that seals the surface. Today gesso

FIG. 6-1 Digital oil painting of Venetian street scene.

is used, but in the past a variety of materials, including rabbit skin glue, was used. Sealing the surface is essential to the longevity of the painting.

A very thick application of paint is often called impasto. Van Gogh was a master of impasto painting. Close examination of his paintings can reveal much about the brushes he used, his color palette, and the quantity of paint on his brush with each application. He used copious amounts of paint on the surface of his paintings. Oil paintings take a very long time to truly dry, often taking nearly a year.

Although canvas surfaces coated with gesso are white in color, many artists will apply a preliminary coating of a thinned-down darker pigment, like raw umber, to establish a middle tone on which to paint. This technique was customary in the old masters' style of painting. On close examination of these paintings in a museum, you will notice that the darker areas of the painting have a very thin application of paint, sometimes almost transparent. The lighter areas of the painting tend to have a more substantial amount of color. This thicker application of paint is much more opaque and is sometimes applied with a palette knife or coarse brush.

In our digital versions of oil painting we will run the gamut from thick impasto painting to more delicate versions that use thin applications of colored glazes. We will be able to simulate the texture of canvas and mimic the strokes that a brush makes on a bumpy surface. Our digital oil paintings will be great candidates for printing on inkjet canvas.

Impasto Technique

Select a photograph that you would like to render as an oil painting with a thick application of paint. Our example is a small still life of pears.

Still lifes continue to be popular. At the height of their popularity, in seventeenth-century northern Europe, they were symbolic of the fragility of life and sometimes contained an insect such as a fly, bee, or butterfly. The inclusion of an insect or a decaying flower additionally spoke of the temporary nature of all living things.

When selecting your base photograph, consider lighting, composition, and color.

Our first task is to make an underpainting, to produce a roughing-in of basic color shapes. Duplicate your Background Layer and use Filter – Artistic – Cutout on the duplicate. You can determine how many colors will be used by

FIG. 6-2 Original photograph of pear still life.

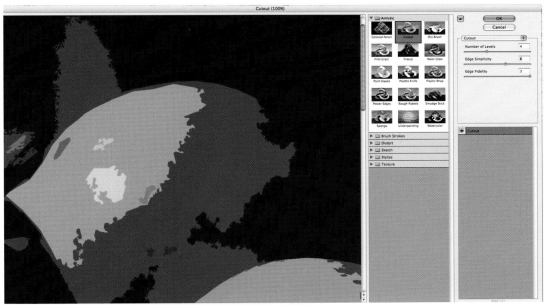

FIG. 6-3 Cutout Filter applied to duplicate layer.

adjusting the Number of Levels slider. We used a high Edge Simplicity and Edge Fidelity.

The Glowing Edges Filter will provide a pencil sketch of the outline or contour edges of the still life. Set the Edge Width at 1 or 2. Use a high Edge Brightness

143

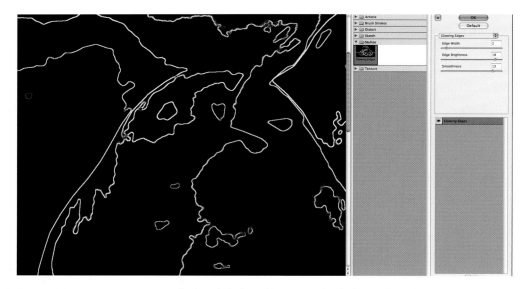

FIG. 6-4 Duplicate the Background Layer again and apply Filter – Stylize – Glowing Edges.

and Smoothness. Now use Image – Adjustments – Invert. Finally, use Image – Adjustments – Desaturate. Set the Blending Mode to Multiply. This Blending Mode makes white disappear, revealing only the sketch outlines.

FIG. 6-5 Terra cotta red outline applied.

On this particular painting I wanted a suggestion of a reddish outline.
I created a new layer and painted a terra cotta red outline around the major
contours of the still life. I used the Pastel on Charcoal Paper Brush from the Dry
Media Brushes Library.

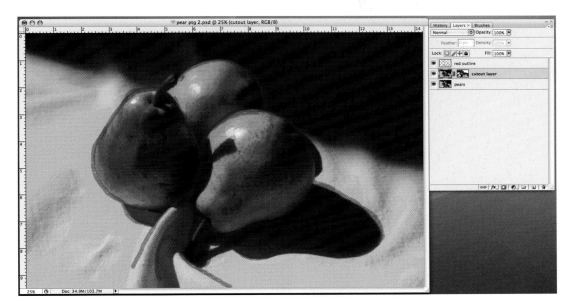

FIG. 6-6 Apply a Layer Mask and brush in the Cut-Out Filter underpainting.

Apply Layer – Layer Mask – Reveal All Mask. Paint with black on the mask,
revealing the Cut-Out Filter rendition. This creates our rough-in of the basic
color shapes.

Select both the Red Outline Layer and the Cutout Layer and create a new
merged layer. Apply Layer – Mask – Hide All Mask. Paint with white to reveal as
much as you like of the underpainting and red line merged layer.

To merge multiple layers into a single new layer, select the layers and hit
Command + Option + E for the Mac or Ctrl + Alt + E on the PC.

Shadow accent colors were added on a new separate transparent layer. (Note
that the layer is made opaque in this illustration so we can better view it. It is
really on a transparent layer; a checkerboard pattern identifies a transparent
layer.)

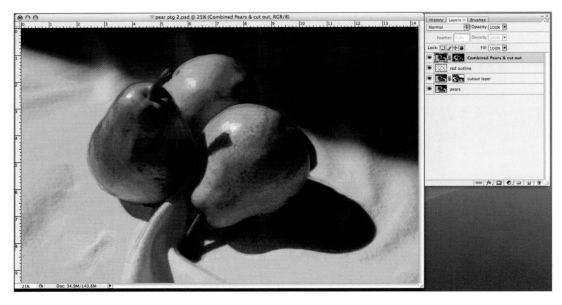

FIG. 6-7 Merged layer with Hide all Mask.

FIG. 6-8 Shadow accent colors added.

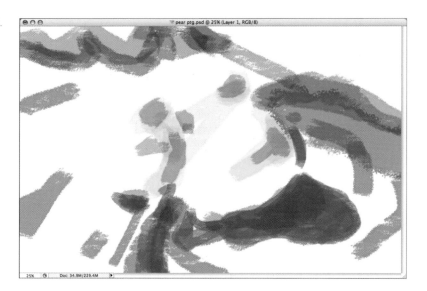

A basic color concept is exaggerated with the addition of a new layer. This new layer is brushed with cool tones in the shadowed areas. The color concept is one of cool colors in the shadow areas and warmer colors in the highlighted areas.

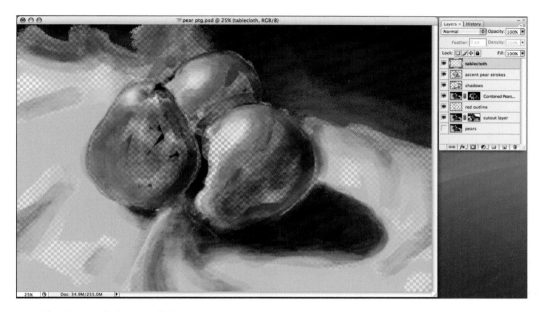

FIG. 6-9 Additional accent color layers are added.

There is no limit to what you can add to the painting. I often use several layers, each with a different area containing accent colors. Here I've added a layer with tablecloth accent colors. Yet another layer was created for accent colors on the pears.

The pencil Sketch Layer has served its purpose and is no longer needed, so it is deleted.

FIG. 6-10 Close-up of painted layers.

I find it helpful to frequently zoom in and check out the application of paint. Did I select the right brush for the job? How opaque or transparent do I want the paint? How loose do I want the painting? These are all artistic considerations that are made throughout the process of painting.

FIG. 6-11 Low-opacity white paint is brushed on a new layer, varying brush size and angle.

Once you are happy with the painting, save a copy in case you have need of it later. Then flatten all your layers together.

In this chapter we will cover a couple of impasto techniques, giving the appearance of a raised paint surface that is rich in paint. In this example we will create a new layer and paint on our brush strokes with a low opacity of white, varying the size and angle of the brush. Try to make the strokes match the contour of the object, like you are massaging the pear with your hands.

In this technique all the strokes are applied in one step and raised or embossed all at once. Use Filter – Stylize – Emboss on the white painted stroke layer. The height was set to 6 pixels. Note that more pixels will result in a higher emboss. The light creating the emboss shadow was directed at an angle of 135 degrees.

The Blending Mode was set on Linear Light for this emboss layer. This particular technique of embossing often resembles a painting with palette knife markings.

FIG. 6-12 Filter – Stylize – Emboss applied.

FIG. 6-13 Linear Light Blending Mode was used.

FIG. 6-14 Pattern added: Canvas texture.

On a real oil painting you will often see the texture of the canvas peeping through in areas where the paint is not as heavy. To simulate this effect, we applied a Pattern Fill. You can add a Pattern Fill Layer from Layer – New Fill Layer – Pattern, or by clicking on the Adjustment Layers icon at the bottom of the Layers Palette, and select Pattern. We chose Canvas from the Artist Surfaces Library. The Pattern Fill Layer was set to the Multiply Blending Mode and the opacity of the layer was set to 35%. Pattern Fill Layers are covered in Chapter 2.

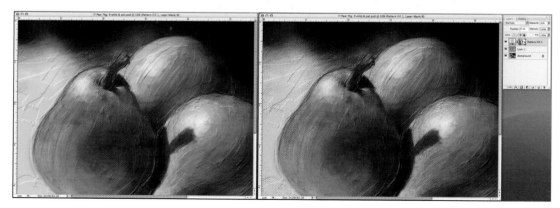

FIG. 6-15 Without and with Canvas Pattern Fill.

The decision to show a little canvas texture is completely reversible. The Pattern Fill comes with a Layer Mask. Stroke with black on the Layer Mask any area that you want to obscure the pattern effect, indicating a thickness of paint. It is not an all-or-nothing technique. You can add as little or as much of the texture that you like. You can also control the opacity of the Pattern Fill.

FIG. 6-16 Completed impasto oil painting with a Palette Knife effect.

Bevel and Emboss Layer Style Oil Painting

The next digital oil painting technique is similar but employs the use of a layer style to achieve the raised texture look of a thickly painted oil painting.

FIG. 6-17 Alaskan vista painted in this technique.

Again, select a photograph that lends itself to paint that will be applied thickly, giving a textural feel. This photo was taken of strawberries on my picnic table after a trip to the pick-your-own fruit stand. The photo was "doctored" a bit in Photoshop to prepare it for the painting process.
A Gaussian blur was used to downplay the background and the wood grain of the table.

FIG. 6-18 Photo of strawberries in a basket.

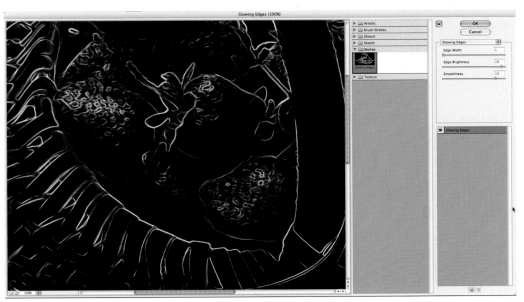

FIG. 6-19 Filter – Stylize – Glowing Edges.

Duplicate the Background Layer. Using the duplicate layer go to Filter – Stylize – Glowing Edges. The sliders were set at 1 for Edge Width, 19 for Edge Brightness, and 13 for Smoothness.

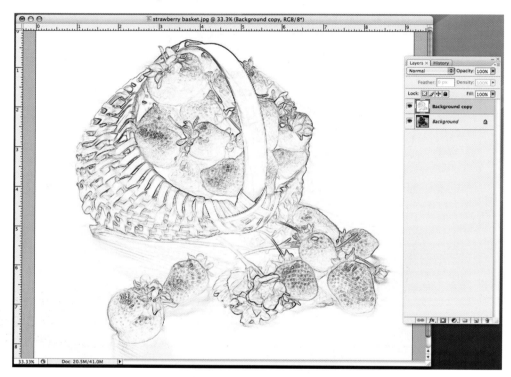

FIG. 6-20 A Sketch Layer is created.

It is easy to turn that bizarre looking Glowing Edges Layer into a sketch effect. Use Layer – Adjustments – Invert and then Layer – Adjustments – Desaturate, and you then have a sketch. It resembles a graphite drawing on white paper.

As we discussed earlier, canvas is often treated with a glaze of a light to medium tone of paint. A medium tone allows the artist to quickly rough-in highlights and shadows, allowing the middle tone to be just that. When working on a white canvas, everything but the highlights need to be painted on the rough-in or underpainting to establish a tonal range. For our strawberry basket we will mimic a linen canvas with a light brown glaze.

Create a new layer and place it above the Background but below the Sketch Layer. Fill it with whatever color you select. Ours is a beige tone. Use Edit – Fill – Foreground (your selected color). The Sketch Layer now needs to have its Blending Mode changed from Normal to Multiply. This mode will make the white disappear, and your sketch is now on the canvas.

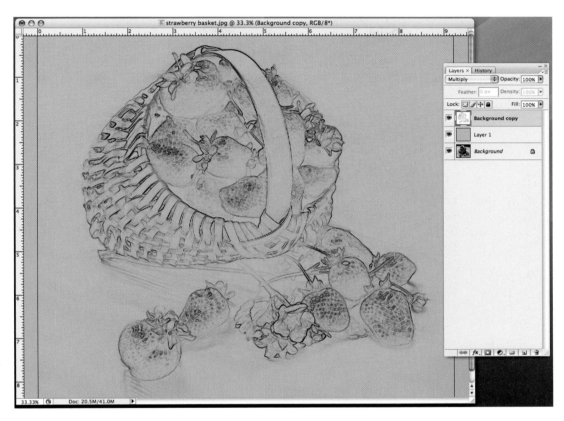

FIG. 6-21 Sketch is applied to a brown linen canvas.

FIG. 6-22 Palette Knife and Paint Daub Filters.

Duplicate the Background Layer again and put it at the top of the layer stack. The task now is to simplify the areas of color, reducing the graduated tones in an attempt to make a strong underpainting. For this example I liked two different filter effects: Palette Knife and Paint Daubs. I liked the blocky color

155

areas produced with the Palette Knife Filter, but I also liked the way the thin strawberry stems were interpreted by the Paint Daub Filter. In short, I liked them both. I wanted a little bit of each one.

To solve this dilemma I copied the background image another time. I applied the Paint Daub Filter to one layer and the Palette Knife Filter to the other layer. Using a mask, I combined the two layers, bringing out the best of both. I then merged down the layer on top, resulting in a layer that had the best of both filters together. I then added a Layer – Layer Mask – Hide All Mask.

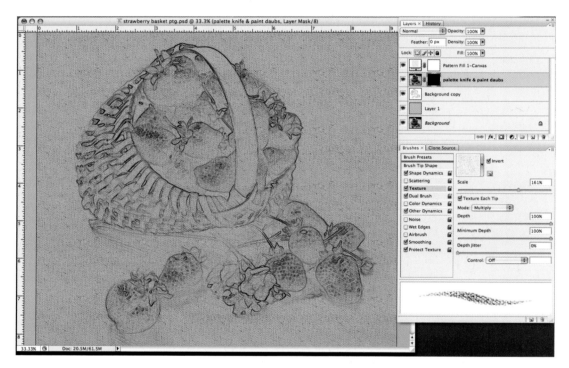

FIG. 6-23 Canvas Texture added with Pattern Fill.

To complete the look of canvas, we added a Pattern Fill. Use Layer – New Fill Layer – Pattern to acquire a Pattern Fill. We selected the Canvas texture from the Artist Surfaces Library of patterns. The Pattern Scale was set to 300%. That scale determines how frequently the pattern will repeat. Note that sizing up can cause a loss of edge fidelity, as would be common in any pixel-based enlargement. The Layer Blending Mode was set to Multiply and the opacity of the layer was lowered to around 50%.

The next step was to select the appropriate brush for the kind of mark that was desired. We selected the brush with Thick Flow Medium Tip from the Wet

Media Brush Library. Next we opened the Brush panel from Windows – Brush. We modified the brush, adding texture, and set the scale of the canvas pattern at 161%.

FIG. 6-24 Roughed-in base of oil painting with Hide All Mask.

Painting white on the mask of the Palette Knife and Paint Daubs Layer, we started to rough-in the color of the painting. A low opacity of around 50% was used, employing short strokes. Vary the size of the brush. I usually use a larger brush for the background and a progressively smaller brush for more detailed areas.

Using Brush Tip Shape from the brush panel I vary the angle of the brush as needed as I paint. It is so nice to have all those possibilities built into one brush. In the real world of oil painting, I would be constantly selecting and alternating different brushes. That would mean a lot more clean-up time at the end of an oil painting session. No paint thinner or turpentine for us, as we are doing it all digitally. We will not be smelling toxic fumes or wiping up paint smears on the surrounding table or easel. We won't be stuck with paint stains under our nails and on our hands and clothing. Hooray for digital!

Try varying the angle (tilt) of the brush and the roundness.

FIG. 6-25 Vary the angle and roundness of the selected brush.

Apply the Layer Mask to that roughed-in paint layer, Palette Knife and Paint Daubs Layer. Duplicate the Background Layer again and place it at the top of the layer stack with a Hide All Mask. Apply a Layer Style of Bevel and Emboss (Layer – Layer Style – Bevel and Emboss). Set the Depth to 3 and Style to Inner Bevel and Smooth. You can determine the angle of light on the ensuing brushwork, if you like, by altering the angle of the global light. Be sure to check the Use Global Light box.

You can select another type of brush, but I stayed with the same one, using more opacity, and began to brush on the impasto paint. Figure 6-26 illustrates what paint was applied in this layer alone. By putting this layer above the Pattern Fill Layer the paint appears thicker, more opaque, and glossier. It covers the texture of the roughed-in areas. Be sure to let some of that show through. Don't overdo it.

A new transparent layer was added to include a few accent colors. This layer also had the same Layer Style of Bevel and Emboss applied. Small touches of paint here can really make a world of difference to the completed painting.

FIG. 6-26 Layer Style of Bevel and Emboss.

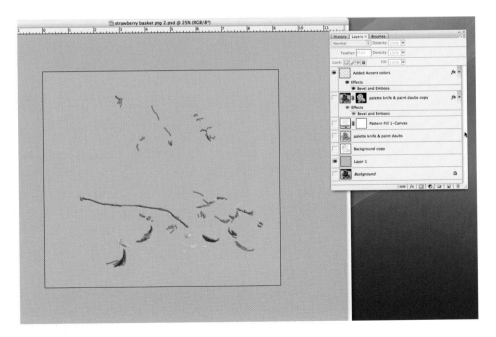

FIG. 6-27 Added accent colors.

FIG. 6-28 Close-up of completed digital impasto oil painting.

FIG. 6-29 Completed digital impasto oil painting.

Portrait Painting Using Bevel and Emboss

Oil paints have traditionally been used throughout the centuries for portraits. Before the invention of photography in 1839, it was the primary way that a loved one could be immortalized. Masters of oil portraiture can command a kingly price for their artistic talents. Our digital version requires less talent, time, and expense.

FIG. 6-30 Original photograph.

Select a photograph that looks like a good candidate for an oil portrait.

As we have done in previous techniques, we will copy the Background Layer by simply dragging the layer to the New Layer icon at the bottom of the Layer Palette. Using that new duplicate layer, we will apply Filter – Glowing Edges. Here, Edge Width was 1, Edge Brightness was 19, and Smoothness was 13.

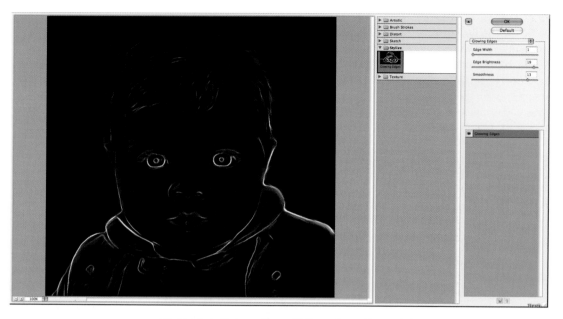

FIG. 6-31 Copied Background Layer with Filter – Glowing Edges applied.

FIG. 6-32 Sketch effect achieved with Multiply Blending Mode.

Add a new layer and use Edit – Fill – Foreground Color to create a base color for the canvas. We used a smoky blue-gray. Place the Glowing Edges Layer above the new colored canvas layer. Using the Glowing Edges Layer, apply Layer – Adjustments – Desaturate and then Layer – Adjustments – Invert. Set the Blending Mode to Multiply.

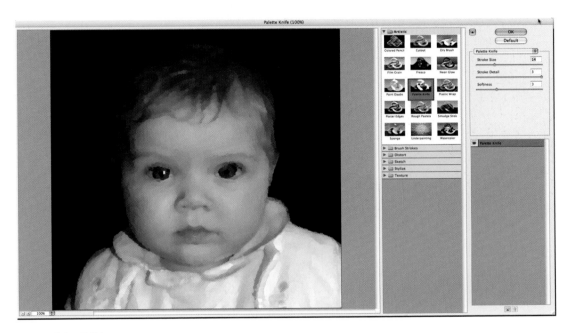

FIG. 6-33 Palette Knife Layer.

Duplicate the Background Layer again and apply Filter – Artistic – Palette Knife. The settings were Stroke Size 14, Stroke Detail 3, and Softness 3. These settings will vary with the size of the file and the detail that you want to retain. We are creating clumps of color.

The next step is to add some texture. We will do that in two ways. The first is to add a Pattern Fill Layer. Select Canvas from the various options. Canvas is found in the Artist Surfaces Library of patterns. Set the Blending Mode to Multiply. The second way is to add texture to our brush. Select the Thick Flow Medium Tip Brush from the Wet Media Brushes Library. Go into the Brushes Palette, found in the Windows menu, and modify that brush. Click on Texture and select Canvas. Set the percentage at 150%. That determines the scale of the texture, and again that number will vary with the size of the file. These numbers are just a suggested starting point. Modify them to suit your particular piece.

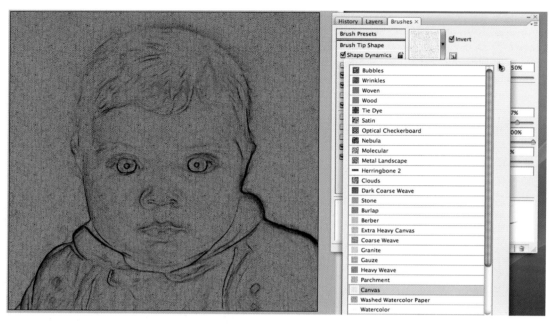

FIG. 6-34 Add a texture, using Pattern – Canvas.

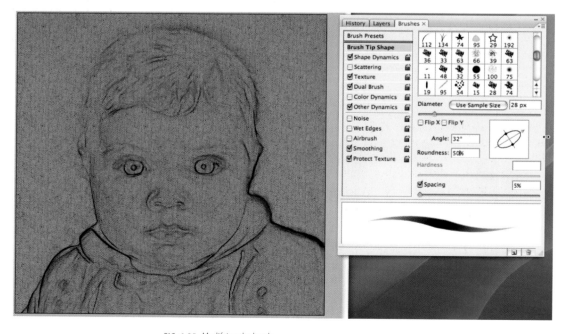

FIG. 6-35 Modifying the brush.

When using an oil painting effect, I'm constantly changing the angle of the brush, applying strokes from various directions, just as would occur with a real stiff-bristled oil painting brush. If you own a drawing tablet and stylus this would be a great opportunity to use it, applying pressure to shape the brush strokes.

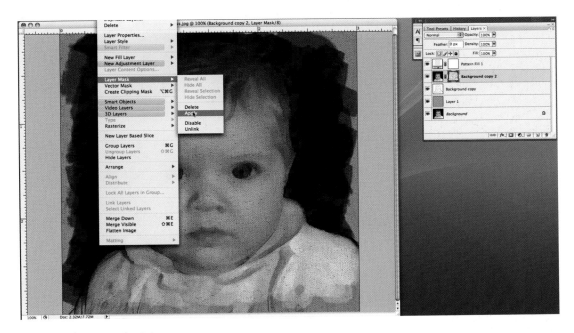

FIG. 6-36 Brushing on an underpainting.

Now go back to that layer that has the Palette Knife Filter applied. Add a Layer – Layer Mask – Hide All Mask. Paint with white on the black mask, at a low opacity, using your custom-made brush. This will reveal the Palette Knife Filter Layer. Vary the size of the brush. I often use a larger brush for the background areas and smaller ones on the face and hair. When you like the effect, apply the Layer Mask.

The painting is rather dark and light in saturation at this stage of the technique.

Duplicate the Background Layer again. Apply the Palette Knife Filter again. Alter the Levels slider in Layer – Adjustments – Levels, creating more contrast

FIG. 6-37 Stacking order of the layers is shown.

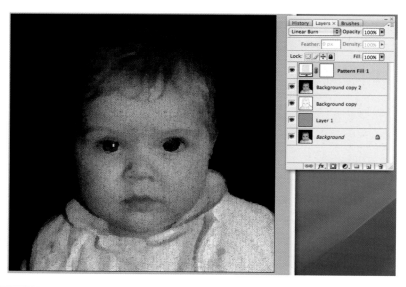

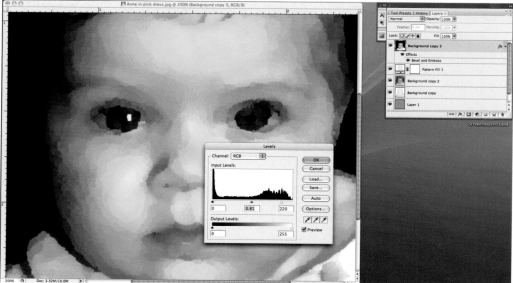

FIG. 6-38 Saturation increased and contrast added in levels.

and saturation. We are preparing to put down larger deposits of pigment in a three-dimensional way.

We put the new layer at the top of the layer stack. This will paint over the pattern texture effect. If you look closely at oil portraits in museums and

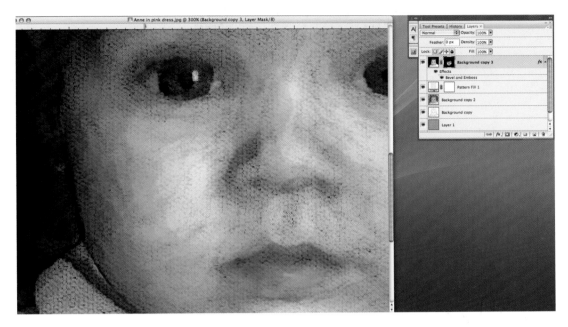

FIG. 6-39 Application of thick paint with the help of a Layer Style.

galleries you will see that the canvas texture only shows through in some areas, usually the dark, shadowed areas. The areas with light colors often have a thicker, more opaque application of paint, obscuring the underlying canvas texture.

Add a Layer Style – Bevel and Emboss. We used Inner Bevel and set the Depth to 2 and the Size and Soften to 0. We used Smooth for the Technique. We added a Layer Mask, hiding all, and painted with white at a moderate opacity (around 35–50%). Use the Rough Round Bristle Brush from the Thick Heavy Brush Library. Build up the paint, allowing canvas to show through in areas, especially in the shadows. You should notice a thickness to the paint application.

This technique really adds the impasto, thick paint application feel.

This technique is great for portraiture, still lifes, and landscapes.

Printing Considerations

Oil painting is, by its very nature, a thick medium and one that is most generally applied to canvas. In the interest of continuing the full oil painting look, I suggest that you investigate the option of printing on canvas. There are some very nice inkjet-coated canvases on the market now. They come both in cut sheets and in a roll.

FIG. 6-40 Completed oil portrait.

Another printing option available is photo labs that offer printing on canvas. Some even offer a "canvas wrap," where the image is placed on inkjet canvas and the canvas is stretched around stretcher bars. A wrap photo shows imagery along the edges of the wrap. Wraps are usually displayed this way, without the use of a traditional frame.

Other printing options include applying the digital oil painting to a gessoed wooden panel. In the interest of print longevity, the panel surface needs to be sealed. The tannic acid that is intrinsic in wood would hasten the demise of any artwork that is exposed to it. Panels were often used in the Renaissance timeframe and even earlier. It is by no means a new concept.

In conclusion, the traditional presentation methods for oil paintings are on canvas or a solid wooden panel. Oil paintings traditionally are framed without glass. Since you will not have the advantage of a UV-filtering glass surface to protect the painting, I would strongly advise the application of a UV deterrent. Golden makes a topcoat of ultraviolet light filters and stabilizers in both a gloss and semi-gloss (www.goldenpaints.com) that can be painted on over

FIG. 6-41 Oil portrait of Sara.

the digital oil painting. These gel topcoats are water-based, so be sure to seal the surface of your ink with a sealer before applying them. There are even some aerosol sprays for UV protection.

Although the methods mentioned above are the most prevalent, you do not need to fall in line with tradition. You can print on metal, handmade papers, other fabrics, and more. The options available to use in this new digital age are ever-increasing. Keep your eyes open for new ways to increase the impact of your work through new printing techniques and materials.

CHAPTER 7

Illustration Techniques in Photoshop

The field of illustration is a very interesting one, and it can use the materials that we have covered thus far. Illustrators tend to be known by their particular style in a specific medium. Illustrators might be recognized for their expertise, for example, in woodcut or airbrush. Illustrations are used in projects as diverse as movie posters, cereal boxes, greeting cards, and magazine articles.

Since we have already covered some basic art mediums, we will concentrate in this chapter on other techniques that might be used for illustrative purposes.

Stylize – Find Edges Illustration Technique

We have already discovered how Photoshop can look at contrast on edges with our Filter –Stylize – Glowing Edges; now we will look at its cousin, Find Edges. Find Edges is a great filter that can be used for the feel of a pencil

FIG. 7-1 Italian tomatoes.

FIG. 7-2 Original photograph from Delft.

sketch. It is not controllable with any sliders, however. We can remedy this a bit after the filter has been used.

As always, find a photograph that you believe is a good candidate for this technique. I chose one from a visit to Delft in the Netherlands.

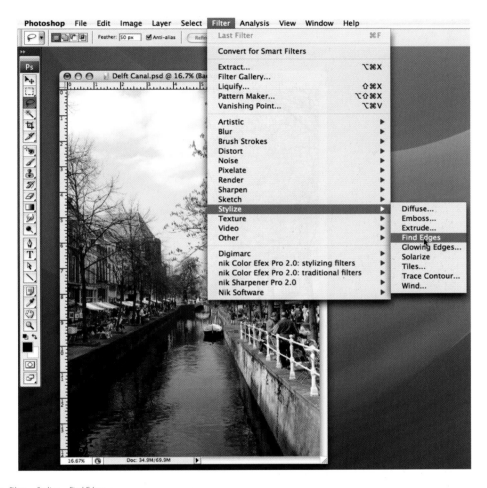

FIG. 7-3 Filter – Stylize – Find Edges.

Duplicate the background and use Filter – Stylize – Find Edges on it.

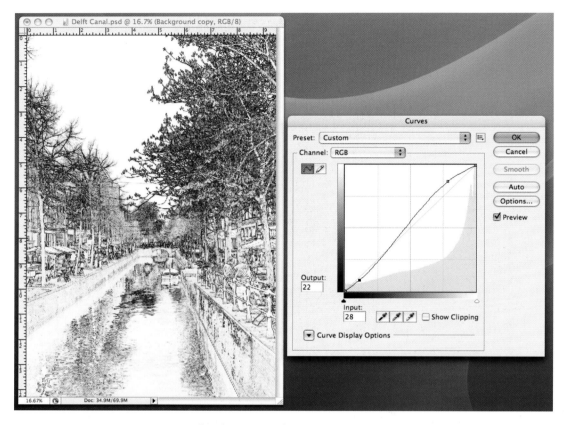

FIG. 7-4 Using Curves to correct the contrast.

Next, use Image – Adjustments – Desaturate. That removes any stray hints of color. Following that, get a Curves Adjustment Layer and tweak that curve to remove small gray areas, pushing the image toward pure black-and-white.

FIG. 7-5 Surface Blur applied.

Duplicate that Background Layer again and place it above the Find Edges Layer. On this new layer, we used Filter – Blur – Surface Blur. The Radius was set to 11 pixels and the Threshold was set to 64 pixels. Those settings will vary with your file size and rendering intent. I wanted to use this filter for a painting effect on the water and sky areas of the illustration.

Next add a Layer – Layer Mask – Hide All Mask on this Surface Blur Layer. The color of this mask will be black and you will paint on it with white to reveal the surface blur effect in specific areas.

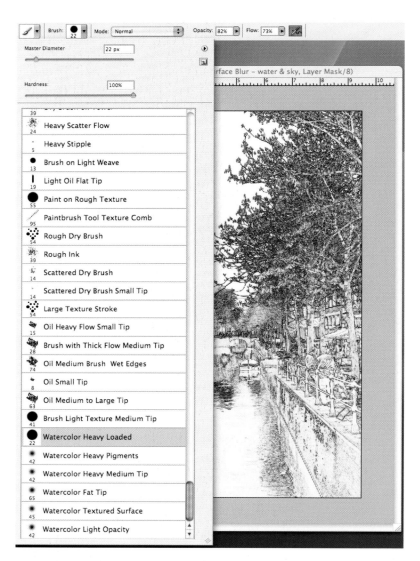

FIG. 7-6 Selecting a brush: Watercolor Heavy Loaded from the Wet Media Brushes Library.

Since I was going for a watery look, I turned to the Wet Media Brushes Library and selected the Watercolor Heavy Loaded Brush.

Using a light opacity, we painted in the water of the canal, leaving some white space. Vary the brush size and opacity throughout this area of painting.

Duplicate that Background Layer yet again. Put it at the top of the layer stack and run the Filter – Blur – Smart Blur on it. This filter deletes detail, by means

FIG. 7-7 Painting the surface blur effect into the illustration using a mask.

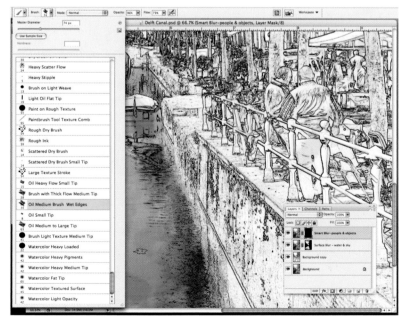

FIG. 7-8 An oil brush is selected to paint in the Smart Blur Layer, featuring the people and buildings.

of the blur, and concentrates the color in patches. Ask again for a Layer – Layer Mask – Hide All Mask. I switched to a different brush from that same Wet Media Brush Library. I chose Oil Medium Brush Wet Edges. I painted, with white paint, on the Hide All Mask, varying the opacity and size of the brush.

FIG. 7-9 Close-up of the painting effect.

The people, buildings, and foliage were predominantly done on the Smart Blur Hide All Layer Mask.

FIG. 7-10 Saturation increased.

To add a little spark, the saturation was increased, using a Hue/Saturation Adjustment Layer.

FIG. 7-11 Before (left) and after (right) black lines were removed from faces on the Find Edges Layer.

On close examination, some of the faces looked weird, with stray black edge lines, from the Find Edges Layer. They were painted out on that layer, using white. While on that Find Edges Layer, some of the sketch-like lines on the outside edges of the illustration were minimized by painting white on that layer.

This illustration used the technique shown above with the Find Edges Filter.

FIG. 7-12 Completed illustration.

FIG. 7-13 Yellow rose illustration.

Faux HDR Illustration

The next technique is a nod at a very popular photo technique called high dynamic range (HDR). There is software marketed to achieve this effect, which merges many photo captures into one, extending the dynamic range of the camera. Usually at least three images, of the same scene, are taken: one metered for the highlights, one metered for the mid-tones, and one metered for the shadows. These images are compiled into one image, thus extending the tonal range of the image. This can be done in Photoshop or with third party software. These images often have a surreal look about them, almost like an illustration.

This faux HDR technique is quick and easy and could be just the ticket for jazzing up a photo. Usually portraits do not fare well with this process.

FIG. 7-14 Image – Adjustments – Shadow/Highlights.

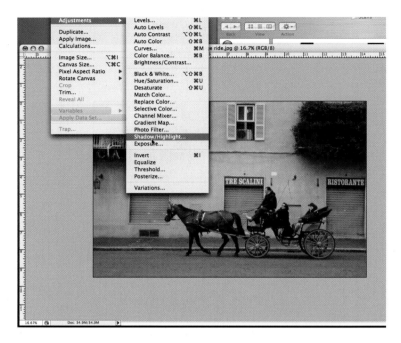

This technique is straightforward and fast. Go to Image – Adjustment – Shadow/Highlights. Use the Show More Options checkbox.

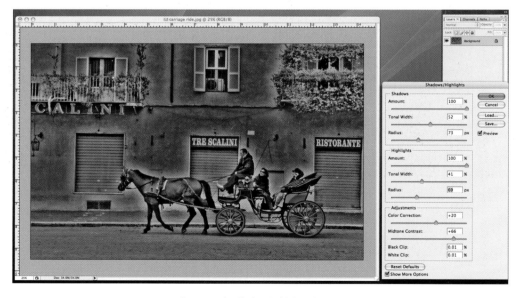

FIG. 7-15 Settings used in Shadow/Highlights Adjustment.

Set the Shadows Amount to 100%. Set the Highlights Amount to 100%. Drag the Midtone Contrast slider until you achieve a good look. Halos may occur, but they can be an interesting effect. Now pull the Tonal Width sliders in both the shadows and highlights until you achieve the look you are going for. Play around with this one. It can be loads of fun on street scenes and other crowded, condensed, and linear-looking photographs.

FIG. 7-16 Illustration and its source photograph.

This photograph of a bike on a canal bridge provided an interesting subject matter for a simulated HDR.

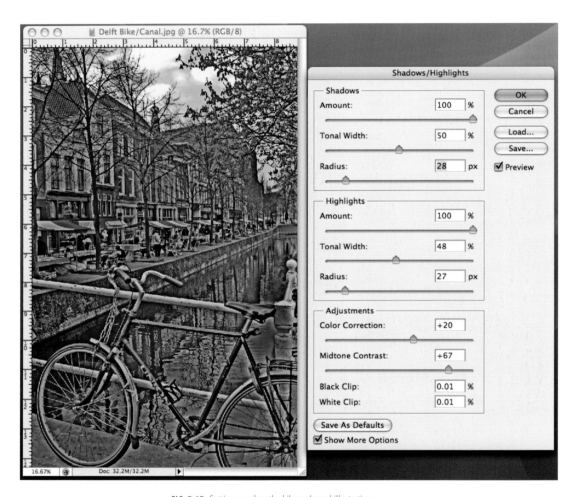

FIG. 7-17 Settings used on the bike and canal illustration.

FIG. 7-18 Faux HDR illustration of infamous Creek Street in Ketchikan, Alaska.

Pen-and-Ink with Aquatint Illustration

The next illustration combines a couple of different looks. It has a bit of a pen-and-ink component mixed with a little aquatinting. This technique might lend itself to book cover illustrations, greeting cards, and magazine illustrations. It has graphic feel combined with a fine art approach.

FIG. 7-19 Original photograph of Dutch lane and bicycle.

First, select a photograph. Ours was a little lane in a Dutch village, with a bike resting near a doorway. The leaning walls of the homes and the ceramic tiled roofs accent the placement of the bicycle in the composition.

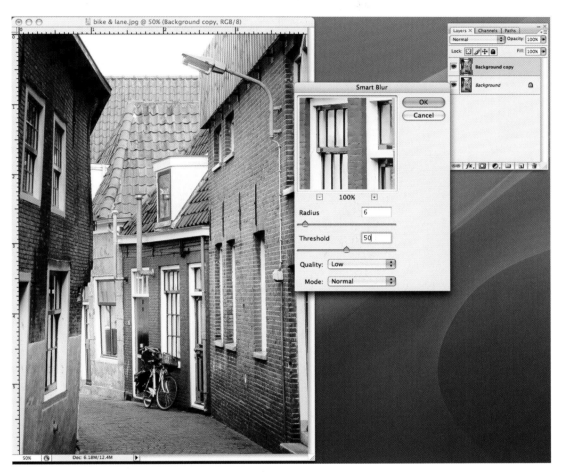

FIG. 7-20 Duplicate Layer using Filter – Blur – Smart Blur.

Duplicate the Background Layer and apply Filter – Blur – Smart Blur. The settings used were a Radius of 6 and a Threshold of 50.

FIG. 7-21 Add a new layer.

Add a new layer between the existing two layers. Edit – Fill with white.

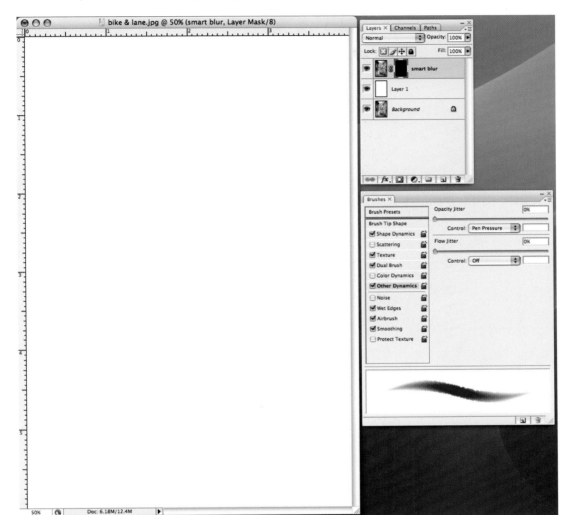

FIG. 7-22 Select a brush; modify the brush.

We will be painting with white on the Hide All Mask. The brush type used is very important. We selected the watercolor Heavy Medium Tip Brush from the Wet Media Brush Library. If you are using a pressure sensitive tablet, like a Wacom tablet, you will want to pull down the Brush menu and adjust the settings for a tablet. Under Other Dynamics the Opacity Control was set to Pen Pressure.

Add a Layer – Layer Mask – Hide All Layer Mask to the Smart Filter Layer.

FIG. 7-23 Filter – Brush Strokes – Ink Outlines.

Duplicate the Background Layer again and put it on the top of the stack. Use Image – Adjustments – Desaturate, reducing the image to a black-and-white photo. On that layer use Filter – Brush Strokes – Ink Outlines. The settings used were Stroke Length 15, Dark Intensity 5, and Light Intensity 40.

FIG. 7-24 Select Color Range.

Using the Eyedropper tool select an area of solid black on this new layer. Go to Select – Color Range. Choose White Matte and set the Fuzziness slider to 175. Select Invert. Now the white is selected. Delete the white. Set the Blending Mode on that layer to Hard Light.

FIG. 7-25 Start to paint with white on the Hide All Mask.

Now, return to the Smart Blur Mask. Begin to paint with white on the mask at a low opacity (20–30%) using the brush we selected earlier.

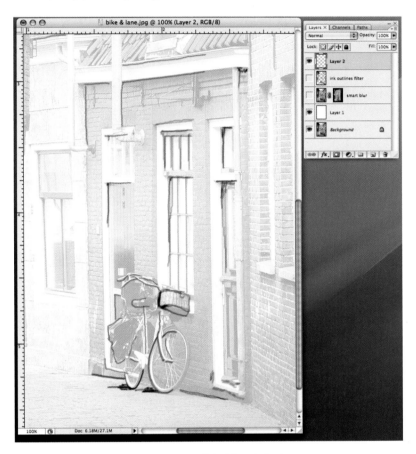

FIG. 7-26 Additional emphasis given to the image with the Calligraphy Brush.

To add a little extra punch to the ink drawing, we created a new transparent layer and drew accent lines with a Calligraphy Brush at 100% opacity, using black. The underlying two layers were turned "off" (Eyeball icon clicked), making them temporarily invisible. We used an oval brush from the Calligraphy Brush Library and set the pixel size at 5 pixels. The Blending Mode remained at Normal.

FIG. 7-27 Another duplicate layer with Glowing Edges.

Duplicate the Background Layer again. Place it above the ink outlines layer but below the added calligraphy outlines. Use the Filter – Stylize – Glowing Edges Filter. Use Image – Adjustments – Desaturate and then Image – Adjustments – Invert. Set this new layer's Blending Mode to Multiply.

FIG. 7-28 Added color accents.

An additional layer was added and the Blending Mode was set to Color. On this layer we painted a few pale accent colors to warm up a few surfaces and add a bit of color to the cobblestone street.

The last touch was to add a Hue/Saturation Adjustment Layer on top of the layer stack. We increased the saturation to make the colors a bit brighter.

FIG. 7-29 Completed illustration.

Dreamy Soft Focus Effect

This next illustration effect is great for a dreamy or romantic kind of feel. It works well on brides, portraits, and landscapes. In some ways it is reminiscent of a soft focus filter that is placed in front of your camera lens. It yields a softness, but it can be controlled by selectively applying the effect. This selectivity allows you to keep a bride's eyes or smile sharp, with a dreamy look elsewhere on the image. It is easy and effective.

FIG. 7-30 Original photograph.

This photograph taken at a historic inn and restaurant caught that magnificent last golden light of the day, prior to sunset. It is a perfect candidate for the Dreamy Soft Focus Effect.

FIG. 7-31 Duplicate layer with Gaussian Blur Filter.

Duplicate the Blur Layer. Use Filter – Gaussian Blur on it. We used 9 for the Pixel Range, but that will vary by the size of your file and the amount of blur that you want. Set the Blending Mode to Darken. Set the layer opacity at around 45%.

FIG. 7-32 Duplicate the duplicate!

Duplicate that duplicate layer. Set the Blending Mode to Lighten and the opacity at around 65%.

It is that simple!

FIG. 7-33 Completed Dreamy Soft Focus Effect.

The final step is to erase anywhere on the duplicate layers where you want to see through to the original sharpness. This can also be achieved, nondestructively, with a Layer Mask.

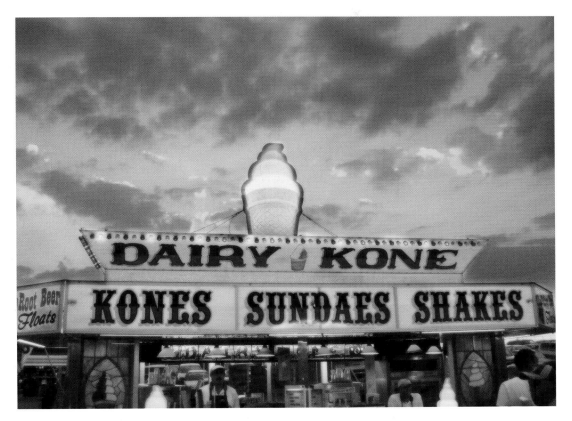

FIG. 7-34 Carnival example of a Dreamy Soft Focus Effect.

CutOut Illustration

This illustration effect will yield an image that will remind you of paint-by-the-numbers kits. It relies on two filters to achieve that look. Colors are simplified down to blocks of similar tones using the CutOut Filter, and a black outline surrounding these color blocks is applied, using Stylize Glowing Edges.

FIG. 7-35 Original photograph of leeks in an outdoor market.

These leeks were found at an outside market in Palermo, Sicily. The stuccoed wall was a fitting background for the beautiful shape of these vegetables.

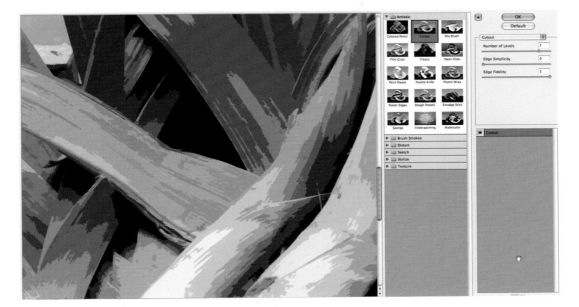

FIG. 7-36 CutOut Filter.

Duplicate the layer and apply Filter – Artistic – CutOut. We used 7 for Levels of Color, 0 for Edge Simplicity, and 3 for Edge Fidelity. In some ways this type of illustration resembles the breakdown of color groupings in preparation for a multicolored silk screen. Silk screening requires a separate screen for each color. The use of many colors requires extreme perfection in the registration of each screen, to precisely sync with previous colors. Photoshop could be used to separate colors for an intended silkscreen project.

Duplicate the Background Layer again and apply Filter – Stylize – Glowing Edges to this second duplication of the beginning or background image. An Edge Width of 1 was used with an Edge Brightness of 20 and a Smoothness of 15. Then use Edit – Adjustments – Invert and Image – Adjustments – Desaturate.

FIG. 7-37 Glowing Edges Filter.

FIG. 7-38 Double-filter effect.

To reinforce the outline feel, making it a bit bolder, the final layer was duplicated and placed at the top of the layer stack.

FIG. 7-39 Completed cutout illustration.

Where is the line between illustration and fine art? That is a discussion that has been evolving for a couple hundred years. If the intended piece of art is destined for a commercial application, it has often been deemed less worthy. Our modern times have seen the validation as art of illustrations by the likes of Norman Rockwell, N.C. Wyeth, and other fine artist/illustrators. It is up to you to draw that fine point for yourself.

I've chosen to include some illustrative techniques in this book. In some instances they are more graphic and less painterly, but in my eyes, worthy of inclusion, all the same.

FIG. 7-40 Illustration of market vegetables (example of Stylize – Find Edges Illustration Technique found on page 171).

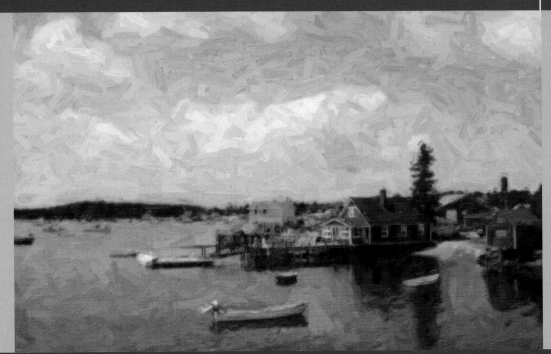

CHAPTER 8

Effects Using Third-Party Software as Photoshop Plug-ins

Filters are great. They can enhance colors, contrast, and mood. They are easy and they are fun to use. They save time that would be better spent writing an action for Photoshop. In short, they are wonderful.

Having said all that, I must say that I seldom, if ever, use a filter universally on an image without some modification. I like to paint the effect on myself, where I want it. I really don't want a global application of an effect.

Despite the huge range of filters available in Photoshop, which are shipped as part of the program, there is still a market for more. There are many fine companies that sell third-party filter software that can be installed in

FIG. 8-1 Vinyl Haven, Maine Harbor, painted with Alien Skin's Snap Art Oil Painting.

Photoshop as plug-ins. I'll cover only a few of my favorites from several companies. You should try some out, including the free ones available on the Internet.

These filter modifications can prepare a photograph for implementation of a painting technique, or they can enhance the image for further painting creativity.

Nik Color Efex Pro 3.0

Nik Color Efex Pro 3.0 offers a wide variety of high-quality filters. The software has an excellent interface and is quite easy to use in Photoshop.

FIG. 8-2 Original photograph of Sicilian landscape.

Our first photograph was taken in Sicily, and although the composition and subject matter were fine, I thought the color could be enhanced for a richer look.

The first task was to warm up the color of the stone wall in the foreground. We chose the Brilliance/Warmth Filter.

Notice the warm, peach-colored color swatch in the bottom right-hand corner, indicating the overlaying color. We also used a light application of this tone in the lighter sky areas, using a Hide All Mask.

FIG. 8-3 Brilliance/Warmth Filter.

FIG. 8-4 Foliage Filter #3. The grass and trees are color enhanced.

The hillside of green was made more attractive with a filter, not fertilizers.

FIG. 8-5 Graduated Filter – Set #3. The sky is enhanced.

Finally the sky is exaggerated with the use of the Graduated Filter. This filter deposits an overlay of color and gradually diminishes the color.

Each layer represents a duplicated Background Layer with a filter applied. A Layer Mask was added to each layer to control where the filter effect would be painted onto the image. The technique used was a soft edged round brush stroking white onto a Hide All Layer Mask.

FIG. 8-6 Stacking of layers in the completed photograph enhancement, using three filters selectively.

FIG. 8-7 Completed enhanced photograph.

FIG. 8-8 Original photograph of nesting birds.

In this case, the original photo was too similar in color tone. Our idea was to warm up some sections of the photograph and cool down other sections with the opposite end of the color wheel.

FIG. 8-9 Colorize — Method #6 to warm up parts of the photograph.

The Colorize Filter was a great way to warm up the birds and some of the vines and grasses.

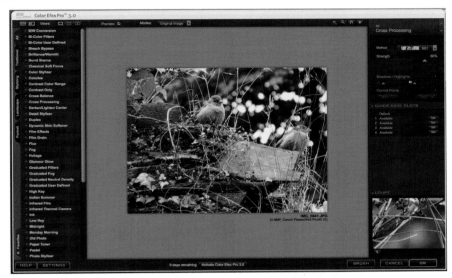

FIG. 8-10 Cross Processing B01 Filter was used to cool areas of the photograph.

The rocks and background areas needed a little cooling. The Cross Processing Filter set to the B01 method was perfect for the job.

FIG. 8-11 Stacking order of filtered layers.

The Cross Processing Filtered Layer was set to 45% opacity. The Colorize Layer was set to 69% opacity.

FIG. 8-12 Completed "filtered" photograph.

Perhaps real bird watchers will object to colorizing the birds, but the impact of the photograph has been improved for a potential painting.

FIG. 8-13 Original photograph of costumed ladies.

This photograph suggested a bygone time and needed a bit of a dreamy, historic feel. Our goal was to ready the photo for an impressionist painting approach.

FIG. 8-14 Polaroid Transfer Filter.

The Polaroid Transfer Filter gives a greenish cast and a bit of blur. A distinctive Polaroid edge is also apparent with this filter.

FIG. 8-15 Sunshine Filter: Light #2, Prefilter #7.

This filter bestows rays of sunshine on our photograph, increasing the feel of golden light.

FIG. 8-16 Glamour Glow Filter: Glow 90%.

This filter makes the dresses glow and blur and darkens the rear foliage.

Each filtered layer used a Hide All Layer Mask to selectively apply the filter effect on the image.

The photo is now ready for other creative painting choices.

FIG. 8-17 Stacking order of the filtered layers.

FIG. 8-18 Completed "filtered" photograph.

Alien Skin's Snap Art

Alien Skin has a product called Snap Art. This software can be installed as a plug-in in Photoshop. It has an interface that is a definite shortcut for painting digitally. You can use it as an aid in painting or you can use it for a stand-alone "hurry up" project.

Our first example will be an oil painting created in Snap Art.

FIG. 8-19 Original photograph of a Scottish castle entrance.

This photo of a castle, with those massive stones, lends itself to a thick application of paint.

We selected Oil Painting as the type of art medium. We duplicated the Background Layer twice. On the first background copy we used the Brush,

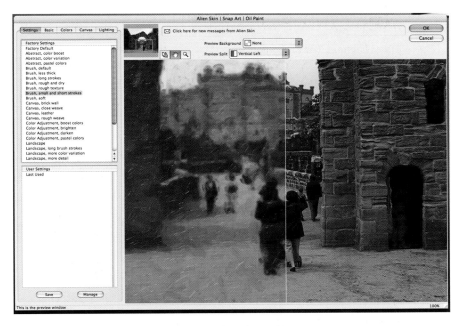

FIG. 8-20 The Snap Art option appears in your Filters menu bar and opens the program.

Small and Short Strokes option. On the other background copy layer we applied the Landscape, More Color Variations option, under Oil Paint. We like to use the Split Screen option to view the changes live.

FIG. 8-21 Two different renditions of oil painting were used: Left — Landscape, More Color Variations and Right — Brush, Small and Short Strokes.

We liked the loose and free application of paint on the left side using Landscape, More Color Variations, but more detail was required in other areas of the painting. The second background copy layer gave us much more detail, using the Brush, Small and Short Strokes option. A combination of the two renditions was what we needed. Nearly all oil paintings have some areas that are loose in approach and other sections that are a bit more detailed. That was what we wanted.

FIG. 8-22 The brush selection was narrowed down to the Oil Medium to Large Tip Brush.

To combine these two renditions we needed Layer Masks. The brush to be used on the Layer Mask should match the feel of the renditions, so we chose the Oil Medium to Large Tip Brush from the Wet Media Brush Library (see Fig. 2-16 in Chapter 2).

FIG. 8-23 Stacking order of the layers.

The top layer was the rendition using small, short, more detailed strokes. That layer had a Hide All Layer Mask attached. The mask was painted with white, using the oil brush mentioned above. That allowed the more detailed rendition to show through in selected areas. The original Background Layer remained intact, in case it was needed later.

We could use this image as a completed work or as a base for the further digital painting.

FIG. 8-24 Completed Alien Skin's Snap Art oil painting.

Combination of Mediums Using Alien Skin's Snap Art

Of course, you can combine anything and see what happens. Sometimes I just meander around with no real concept in place, just experimenting. These forays into "what-if" possibilities are often fruitful and are always fun. Just follow your instincts and see where it might take you.

In the next example we'll incorporate pencil sketches with pointillism, oil pastels, and impasto. That is a very unlikely scenario for a real painting, but in the digital world we do not need to conform to a singular look or medium. Our only goal is to make something pleasing to our eyes.

This photograph became a trial image for a variety of filters, which we would later combine.

FIG. 8-25 Original photograph of a windmill.

FIG. 8-26 Snap Art Filters: Impasto, Pencil Sketch, Oil Pastels, and Pointillism.

The Background Layer was copied four times. The Pointillism Filter used the Assorted Pastels, No Color Variation option. The Pastels Layer used the Portrait, Oil Pastels option. The Pencil Sketch Layer used the Assorted, Sketchy and Medium Coverage option. And, finally, the Impasto Layer used the Assorted, More Detail option.

FIG. 8-27 The stacking order of the filtered layers.

The Pointillism Layer was set at 100% opacity; the Oil Pastel Layer was set at 68% opacity; and the Pencil Sketch Layer was set at 55% opacity and a Blending Mode of Multiply. The Impasto Layer was set at 53% opacity and some areas were masked out. The masking was done on the end walls and was not a complete mask. A brush with a 43% opacity of black, painted on the mask, allowed some of the impasto texture to remain.

FIG. 8-28 The completed combination of mediums windmill.

Ben Vista's PhotoArtist 2

The Ben Vista PhotoArtist 2 program has a wide range of art mediums and variations in those categories, which can be applied with adjustable opacity (measured in 10% increments) and with different size brushes.

FIG. 8-29 The PhotoArtist 2 interface.

FIG. 8-30 This compilation painting was made from a variety of filters.

Filters used in the image in Figure 8-30 included Watercolor, Impressionist, and Erosion. This software is simple to use and has a nice range of art materials.

Filters are another set of tools to add to your artistic tool belt. As I've mentioned, I seldom use a filter for a global effect, but instead apply a filter where the effect is desired. I don't want the image to look like it has gone through a filter process. Again, experimentation is needed to fine-tune your look.

I encourage you to try a variety of filter techniques. Put each one on a separate layer so that everything is reversible and nondestructive. Play with the abandon of a child with a new set of toys. That is how new discoveries are made.

In Conclusion

It has been my pleasure to share digital painting techniques with you. The field of digital painting is just beginning. You are indeed a pioneer. I hope, as I stated in Chapter 1, that you have taken off your digital safety belt and have enjoyed exploring the digital painting techniques in this book.

Change is one of the things that you can count on in life. As Photoshop continues to evolve and change, new digital painting techniques will emerge. Printers of the future will offer new possibilities. New papers, inks, and digital materials will offer possibilities we can't imagine now.

I can still remember the thrill when, in 1984, I purchased my first Macintosh computer and black-and-white printer. A color computer screen was still in the future. The computer had only 128 K of memory and had a screen the size of an index card. The dot matrix printer used only standard white paper with black ink. Inkjet printers and colored inks were still in the future. My first scanner, the Thunderscan, only scanned in black-and-white, and took about fifteen minutes to make a scan, with pixels the size of Mt. Everest. Flatbed scanners and film scanners were still in the future.

All of this is to say, "Who knows what the future will bring?" Keep experimenting. In the wet darkroom I mixed chemical concoctions and put my own emulsions on artists' papers, working in some nontraditional ways, creating my own photographic paper. Now, in the digital darkroom, I'm applying inkjet coatings on various artists' papers and substrates, making my own inkjet papers and canvases. Times change. The materials change. The artistic possibilities expand. It is for you, the artist and photographer, to continue to change, explore, and evolve with these new materials. The art is inside you. These materials just offer new possibilities to express that art.

With any kind of luck, I should be able to rewrite this book five years from now with new techniques and possibilities that are as yet unknown. Isn't it wonderful to be part of this new digital artistic medium? I look forward to sharing this digital artistic journey with you.

Index